TEACHER'S MANUAL

INTRODUCTION

Legal Ethics is a comprehensive book, and intentionally so. Our goal is to provide a broad array of materials that will allow teachers to construct a wide variety of courses. We have combined the most popular formats for the professional responsibility course – hypothetical problems, statutory and doctrinal analysis, and interdisciplinary readings – and added concise summaries of legal and ethical rulings, original commentary, full-length case studies, and extensive references. Our rationale for this diverse set of materials is that there has been relatively little consensus on what a class in professional responsibility should look like. Some professors emphasize the law of lawyering and some primarily address the formal rules and substantive areas where case law is most developed. Others are more interested in normative issues concerning lawyers' roles. Some classes will devote significant attention to the regulation of the profession; others will stress individual attorney conduct. Curricular offerings also vary considerably in scope and format. Materials that work well in an elective three unit seminar may be too extensive for a large two-unit required course. For some individuals, interdisciplinary materials may seem essential, for others, a distraction. Our aim has been a book that can be adapted to meet all these needs.

Most professional responsibility teachers whom we know have supplemented conventional doctrinal materials with handouts from diverse sources including fiction and journalism, as well as the increasingly rich scholarship on legal ethics and the legal profession. This book is a direct descendant of our own sets of handouts, and (like many law textbooks) grew partly out of our self-interested desire to avoid tedious pre-semester editing work. Obviously, we do not promise that you will never cut and paste again, but we hope to minimize the burden by including many of the most popular readings and a diverse sampling of other materials in a single text. For this reason, we have tried to err on the side of inclusiveness.

No teachers in an ordinary two- or three-credit legal ethics course will be able to cover all the material in the textbook. For this reason, this manual offers suggestions about what to cut from each chapter if the schedule leaves time for only a bare-bones treatment of the topic.

Changes in the Fifth Edition

Our main objective in this edition was to bring discussion of the law and the Model Rules of Professional Conduct up to date, and include materials on the recent controversies, such disputes over the scope of confidentiality protections, the regulation of advertising, and lawyers' role in formulating the federal government's war on terror and policies on torture of political prisoners. Since almost no jurisdictions adhere to the Model Code of Professional Responsibility, we have dropped most Code references from the text. At the same time, we have eliminated – not without regret – some materials that have lost their salience.

The Use of Discussion Questions

Throughout the book we have organized our notes and commentary around discussion questions. Most are set off by numbers, while a few are integrated directly into the text. We have tried to avoid rhetorical or leading questions. Instead, we flag open issues, points of current controversy, and conceptual or empirical difficulties with the arguments presented in the readings. In an important sense, these questions are the real teacher's manual: we have used them successfully to lead discussions in our own classes, and our best advice to a teacher who is uncertain how to discuss some of the readings is simply to begin with these questions.

Structuring the book around open questions serves another purpose as well. In our view, legal ethics is a dynamic subject – a subject in which fundamental doctrinal issues, like the professional ideals they mirror, are in a state of flux. Although the ABA Code and Model Rules (and now the *Restatement*) have given some measure of stability to lawyers' professional obligations, we believe that it is profoundly misleading to teach the course as if these professional standards have resolved all important questions. To treat many areas as settled doctrine runs the risk of obscuring crucial ethical and policy issues lurking below the surface of the rules. Worse, it runs the risk of marginalizing students' own ideals and sense of judgment, the very capacities that an ethics course is meant to develop.

By presenting topics as first and foremost a set of thought-provoking questions, we hope to avoid the twin pitfalls of intellectual complacency and

TEACHER'S MANUAL

LEGAL ETHICS

FIFTH EDITION

by

DEBORAH L. RHODE
Ernest W. McFarland Professor of Law
Director, Stanford Center on the Legal Profession
Stanford Law School

DAVID LUBAN
University Professor
Professor of Law and Philosophy
Georgetown University Law Center

FOUNDATION PRESS

2009

Mat #40775996

© 2009 By THOMSON REUTERS/FOUNDATION PRESS
195 Broadway, 9th Floor
New York, NY 10007
Phone Toll Free 1–877–888–1330
Fax (212) 367–6799
foundation–press.com

Printed in the United States of America

ISBN 978–1–59941–597–0

TEXT IS PRINTED ON 10% POST CONSUMER RECYCLED PAPER

uncritical formalism. No doubt some students, particularly those who have low tolerance for ambiguity, will occasionally become uncomfortable with our message that much of legal ethics is a subject of questions rather than of answers.

But the class as a whole will often benefit most from open-ended discussions in which reaching an ultimate resolution is neither possible nor the point. Of course, some questions have clear doctrinal answers, or at least a small range of possible answers. One purpose of this Manual is to supply those answers wherever we believe they exist, and to spell out in detail any that are especially complex.

As a result, professors will find that some problems and questions receive extensive treatment in this Manual while others do not. This reflects our best judgment of which issues professors may wish to have addressed as well as which topics offer opportunities for colorful examples and humorous details that are not included in the text. When we provide no answer to a discussion question, it is generally because we believe that the answer is obvious or that the question is open to a range of responses.

A Note on the Footnotes

Legal Ethics includes footnoted reference material that provides helpful bibliographic assistance and reinforces the message that many ethical issues are a matter of practical importance and professional controversy. We hope that some readers will find the questions sufficiently interesting to pursue further research. In addition, we hope to assist scholarship by both faculty and students and to facilitate teachers' class preparation. In the current edition, however, we have deliberately cut back on the footnotes, in order to direct students more effectively to the most promising sources on each topic and make the book more user friendly. In addition, when in our opinion a single article provides the best introductory supplement, we have flagged it for special attention.

Where relevant to the discussion, *Legal Ethics* identifies certain videos, documentaries, and other innovative ethics materials that we have found useful.

A note is in order concerning our treatment of our own writing on issues of legal ethics. One of our over-all goals for the book is to present a fair representation of scholarly opinion on important issues of legal ethics. As active participants in many of the scholarly discussions of these issues, we concluded that it would be counterproductive to exclude our own work. At the same time, it is never our intention to ram our own views down the student's throat. The procedure we have followed is instead to treat ourselves "in the third person": we include excerpts from, or references to, our own writings where it seems to us that these excerpts fairly present a point of view that is significant in current debates. But we treat these excerpts no differently than we would similar excerpts by other authors, and we encourage readers to think about them skeptically and critically. Students should feel free to object to our views and to suggest that we are completely wrongheaded. We are always happy to hear from professors who are interested in our response or who have suggestions for modifying the text in its next edition.

SAMPLE SYLLABI FOR 2- AND 3-HOUR CLASSES

The syllabi included here are modeled on versions of the course that we have taught. For convenience, we reference the reading assignments by chapter and section. Some of the sections include more pages than it is realistic to assign. Professors should determine which readings to omit from lengthy sections. Since this is very much a matter of individual taste, we have not identified omissions on the syllabi. However, the suggestions for a "bare bones" treatment that we provide at the beginning of each chapter of this Manual should provide some guidance.

Professors will notice that these syllabi omit some chapters entirely. We like to "rotate" chapters in and out of our course outlines from year to year in order to avoid the staleness that comes from repeating the identical course. Thus, it is perfectly plausible to substitute unassigned chapters into these course outlines, as we ourselves do.

14-WEEK, 2 HOUR CLASS

Week 1: INTRODUCTION
> Assignment: Introduction.

Week 2: THE LEGAL FRAMEWORK OF LAWYERS' ETHICS--SELF-REGULATION AND THE CODES
> Assignment: Chapter III, Sections B and C. Skim the ABA Model Rules of Professional Conduct.

Week 3: CONCEPTIONS OF THE LAWYER'S ROLE (I)
> Assignment: Chapter IV, sections A-D.2

Week 4: CONCEPTIONS OF THE LAWYER'S ROLE (II)
> Assignment: Chapter IV, section E (*Cueto* and/or "Lawyers for Terrorists"); plus either the discovery abuse material or *Lee*.

Week 5: CONFIDENTIALITY AND THE ATTORNEY-CLIENT PRIVILEGE (I)
> Assignment: Chapter V, Problem 1, Sections A and C.1-C.2. Film, "Ethics on Trial," first segment (about 10 minutes).

Week 6: CONFIDENTIALITY AND THE ATTORNEY-CLIENT PRIVILEGE (II)
> Assignment: Chapter V, Sections D and E.

Week 7: DILEMMAS OF ADVOCACY
> Assignment: Chapter VI, Sections B and C.

Week 8: THE COUNSELING FUNCTION[1]
> Assignment: Chapter IX. A plus one or more of the following sections (corporate practice, family practice, tax practice, government lawyers). Distribute instructions for Week 9 negotiation exercise. Pair up with a partner, and perform the negotiation exercise outside of class.

---

[1]Alternatively, professors may wish to omit Chapter IX and use material from Chapter VII.

Week 9: NEGOTIATION AND MEDIATION
Assignment: Chapter VIII, sections A and B.

Week 10: CONFLICT OF INTEREST (I) – CONCURRENT CONFLICTS
Assignment: Chapter X, Sections A and C.

Week 11: CONFLICT OF INTEREST (II) – FORMER-CLIENT CONFLICTS
AND IMPUTED DISQUALIFICATION
Assignment: Chapter X, Sections D and E.

Week 12: LAWYER-CLIENT DECISION MAKING[2]
Assignment: Chapter XI.

Week 13: MARKET REGULATION
Assignment: Chapter XII, Sections A, B, and either sections D, E, or F.

Week 14: THE DISTRIBUTION OF LEGAL SERVICES; ACCESS TO JUSTICE AND PRO BONO REPRESENTATION
Assignment: Chapter XIII, Sections B, E and G.

---

[2] Professors may wish to omit this unit and substitute either an additional class on conflicts of interest, or an additional class on market regulation.

14-WEEK, 3 HOUR CLASS

(divided into one one-hour and one two-hour class period)

Week 1, **class 1** (one hour each week): INTRODUCTION
    Assignment: Introduction

Week 1, class 2 (two hours each week): IMAGES OF THE LAWYER'S ROLE
    Assignment: ABA Model Rules of Professional Conduct 1.2, 1.3.
    Film: "Ethics in America: To Defend a Killer".

Week 2, class 1: THE LEGAL FRAMEWORK OF LAWYERS' ETHICS--SELF-REGULATION AND THE CODES
    Assignment: Chapter III, Sections B and C. Skim the ABA Model Rules of Professional Conduct.

Week 2, class 2: AN INTRODUCTION TO THE DISCIPLINARY SYSTEM
    Assignment: Chapter XV, Sections A, B, and C or A, C, and E.

Week 3, class 1: CONCEPTIONS OF THE LAWYER'S ROLE
    Assignment: Chapter IV, Sections A and B.

Week 3, class 2: THE ADVERSARY SYSTEM
    Assignment: Chapter IV, Sections C and D.

Week 4, class 1: PROSECUTORIAL ETHICS[3]
    Assignment: Chapter VI, Section D.

Week 4, class 2: CRIMINAL DEFENSE
    Assignment: Chapter VI, Sections A, B, and C.

Week 5, class 1: ALTERNATIVES TO NEUTRAL PARTISANSHIP
    Assignment: Chapter IV, Section E.

Week 5, class 2: RULE 11, DISCOVERY ABUSE, AND INCIVILITY
    Assignment: Chapter IV, Section F.

Week 6, class 1: CONFIDENTIALITY AND THE ATTORNEY-CLIENT PRIVILEGE (I)
    Assignment: Chapter V, Problem 1, Sections A and B. Film: "Ethics on Trial," the first segment (about 10 minutes).

Week 6, class 2: CONFIDENTIALITY AND THE ATTORNEY-CLIENT PRIVILEGE (II)
    Assignment: Chapter V, Sections C and E.

Week 7, class 1: CONFIDENTIALITY AND THE ATTORNEY-CLIENT PRIVILEGE (III)

---

   [3] We insert the material on criminal prosecution and defense in the middle of the material from Chapter IV in Weeks 3 and 5 because it helps to break up the more abstract and theoretical material on the nature of adversary advocacy with the very concrete and gripping problems of litigation ethics. Moreover, just as the criminal defense function typifies neutral partisanship, the prosecution function typifies (at least in theory) an alternative to neutral partisanship, since prosecutors are enjoined to seek justice, not merely victory.

Assignment: Chapter V, Sections D, F, and G.

Week 7, class 2: THE COUNSELING FUNCTION
Assignment: Chapter IX. A plus one or more of the following sections (corporate practice, family practice, tax practice, government lawyers). Distribute instructions for Week 9 negotiation exercise. Pair up with a partner, and perform the negotiation exercise outside of class, to be discussed in Week 8, class 2.

Week 8, class 1: SUPERVISORY AND SUBORDINATE LAWYERS
Assignment: Chapter VII, Problem 1, plus Sections C and D; *or* Section B (Sarbanes-Oxley).

Week 8, class 2: NEGOTIATION AND MEDIATION
Assignment: Chapter VIII.

Week 9, class 1: CONFLICT OF INTEREST (CRIMINAL DEFENSE)
Assignment: Chapter X, Sections A and B.

Week 9, class 2: CONCURRENT CONFLICTS IN CIVIL CASES
Assignment: Chapter X, Section C.

Week 10, class 1: CONFLICT OF INTEREST (FORMER-CLIENT CONFLICTS AND IMPUTED DISQUALIFICATION)
Assignment: Chapter X, Sections D and E.

Week 10, class 2: OTHER CONFLICTS OF INTEREST
Assignment: Chapter X, Sections F or G; section I.

Week 11, class 1: LAWYER-CLIENT DECISION MAKING (I)[4]
Assignment: Chapter XI, Sections A and B.

Week 11, class 2: LAWYER-CLIENT DECISION MAKING (II)
Assignment: Chapter XI, Section C.

Week 12, class 1: ADVERTISING
Assignment: Chapter XII, Section A.

---

[4] Some professors may wish to omit the material for this week and substitute either additional classes on conflicts of interest or additional classes on the distribution of legal services (see Week 14).

Week 12, class 2: SOLICITATION; UNAUTHORIZED PRACTICE
Assignment: Chapter XII, Sections B and D.

Week 13, class 1: ATTORNEYS' FEES
Assignment: Chapter XII, Section F.

Week 13, class 2: ATTORNEYS' FEES AND THE FINANCING OF LITIGATION
Assignment: Chapter XII, Section G; Chapter X, Section H (on fee-related conflicts of interest).

Week 14, class 1: THE DISTRIBUTION OF LEGAL SERVICES; PRO BONO REPRESENTATION
Assignment: Chapter XIII, Sections B, C and G.

Week 14, class 2: PUBLIC INTEREST LAW
Assignment: Chapter XIII, Sections D and E.

INTRODUCTION

The introduction to the book includes two distinct sections: a discussion of the role of moral philosophy in legal ethics, and an extended case study. "Rita's Case."[5]

Moral Philosophy

Numerous issues in legal ethics echo distinctions and debates in moral philosophy. Yet few professors have either the time or inclination to devote a substantial part of the course to a study of the classics or contemporary ethical frameworks. Most writing in moral philosophy is too abstract to connect directly to legal ethics, and it is often difficult and unduly time consuming to bridge the gap between philosophical

---

[5] "Rita's Case" was originally prepared by the Harvard Program on the Legal Profession, and distributed in typescript form. A shortened and revised version appears in *The Social Responsibilities of Lawyers* 2 (Philip Heymann & Lance Liebman 1988). We have used the original version, which includes several ethical issues that the published version omits.

arguments and the subject of the course.

We believe, however, that is useful to offer a   short self-contained overview, which connects central philosophical debates with key practical issues in professional responsibility. None of these notes require prior philosophical training on the part of either students or professors.

In addition to this summary in the opening chapter, several other sections of the book draw on arguments and distinctions from moral philosophy. Chapter IV raises the question of whether an advocate in the adversary system is obligated to perform actions on behalf of the client that may be ethically objectionable outside of the legal context. We link this question to the philosophical debate between those who regard moral obligations as universal and impartial and those who stress the importance of more particular, role-bound loyalties. Chapter VII addresses the utilitarian underpinnings and moral limits of cost-benefit analysis, since corporate lawyers are often asked to couch their legal advice in cost/benefit terms. In Chapter XI, we refer to the rich philosophical literature on paternalism to address problems in representing clients under a disability, juveniles, and clients with seemingly irrational or self-destructive desires.
Some teachers may wish to postpone reading and discussion of the introductory notes until those portions of the course in which philosophical materials are most clearly relevant. This is a perfectly appropriate way to use the Introduction, which we intend to complement any and all of the later philosophical commentary.

Our reason for starting the book with this section is born of decades of classroom experience. Students return again and again to the same moral issues on which there is a rich philosophical literature. As a preliminary matter, many individuals are curious about whether there is a difference between "ethics" and "morality," and sometimes seem to place great weight on the alleged distinction between the two (though different students have different interpretations of what the distinction is). For all practical purposes, we regard the terms as synonymous, but point out that some philosophers have viewed ethics as customary norms and morality as more abstract, philosophical reflection.

We then turn to the inevitably vexed question about moral relativism. In our view, most students who give voice to relativistic sentiments do so not because they are indeed relativists (we suggest that virtually no one really is), but because they are uncomfortable about the prospect of imposing moral beliefs on others. We therefore offer reassurances that opposition to relativism is not an invitation to moral arrogance or authoritarianism. We also suggest that relativism turns out on reflection to be an unattractive substitute for tolerance. Teachers inevitably confront the question of whether moral standards are "squishy" in comparison with the rigor of substantive law. We often respond by reminding students of the principal lesson of their own educational experience: that many legal questions are every bit as complex and controversial as moral questions.

Finally, we introduce the distinction between utilitarian/consequentialist moral theories, deontological/rights-based moral theories, and virtue-based moral theories -- a distinction that recurs in other portions of the book that incorporate philosophical materials.

Rita's Case

We have found that "Rita's Case" makes a satisfying opening class in professional responsibility; it engages student interest and encourages them to look forward to the remainder of the course. "Rita's Case" also anticipates the topics of several other chapters in the book; by referring back to the Introduction when those topics arise, teachers can impart an extra measure of coherence to the course. The discussion questions highlight the following recurrent themes.

(1) The contrast between Maynard's and Kiladis's approaches to the advocate's role ties in directly with Chapter IV's analysis of neutral partisanship. Maynard's reference to the "lawyer for the situation" also anticipates the corresponding unit in Chapter X on conflicts of interest. The very fact that highly competent and conscientious attorneys can conceive of their role in quite different terms itself conveys a significant message to students: that issues of role definition matter, and cannot be resolved simply by applying codified rules.

(2) Additional issues regarding the moral limits of zealous advocacy arise from the attorneys' efforts to "neutralize" the contributions of other professionals working on the case where those contributions could compromise the client's interests.

13

(3) The question that Kiladis confronts at the end of the case -- how to respond to the possibility of child abuse at the home, points up issues of confidentiality, partisanship, and third party interests that are central to Chapters IV and V.

(4) The entire case graphically raises questions about the appropriateness of the adversary system for resolving disputes where significant interests are unrepresented or badly represented -- a question that recurs in Chapters IV and XIII.

(5) The conclusion of the case presents the very real possibility that Maynard and Kiladis have at the end achieved an outcome for Gladys -- adopting Rita -- that may not have served Gladys' best interest. Judging from her prior life history, it seems likely that what Gladys actually wanted was custody when she was able to cope with Rita, combined with support from social services agencies for times when those coping capacities fell short. Maynard and Kiladis may have judged intuitively that the court would never agree to this outcome and -- perhaps unconsciously -- reinterpreted Gladys's aim on terms that the legal system could deliver: adoption. If so, the case raises crucial problems addressed later. Chapter XIII highlights the problem of public interest lawyers redefining their clients' aims, while Chapter XI deals with paternalism on the part of lawyers toward their clients.

(6) The case also raises concerns of distributive justice that are the focus of Chapter XIII: What legal interests get representation, and why? How can the concerns of those unable to afford legal services be safeguarded?

(7) Finally, "Rita's Case" poses a number of more particular rule-related questions

• What should Kiladis do about Gladys' unreported income? It bears noting that surveys of welfare recipients reveal that well over 90% have unreported income. Since no state sets support payments at a level that could meet recipients' subsistence needs, that is not surprising. But whatever their personal views on the subject (which will probably vary), students should also grapple with how to avoid complicity in fraud.

• What, if anything, should Kiladis do regarding the inadequacies of Rita's lawyer, David Slade? Should she take up her concerns with Slade or the court? How can the effectiveness and accountability of court-appointed counsel be ensured?

• How should Kiladis deal with her suspicion that Gladys's New York guardianship of Rita may not be legally valid in Pennsylvania? (If there was directly adverse legal authority on the point, she had an obligation to disclose it to the court.)

• How serious is it that Kiladis evidently had extensive *ex parte* contacts with Rita as well as with social services officials, all of whom were represented by counsel? The contact with Rita is arguably forbidden by Model Rule 4.2. However, the issue of contact with social services employees is a closer call. Section 101(1) of the *Restatement* permits contacts with "employees of a represented governmental agency or with a governmental officer being represented in the officer's official capacity." However, section 101(2) adds a proviso: "In negotiation or litigation by a lawyer of a specific claim of a client against a governmental agency or against a governmental officer in the officer's official capacity, the prohibition . . . applies, except that the lawyer may contact any officer of the government if permitted by the agency or with respect to an issue of general policy."

• Was it a conflict of interest or fraud on the court to initiate adoption proceedings on behalf of Gladys and Juan when it was clear that their marriage was in the process of dissolution? (Given that Juan might be liable for unwanted child support payments, such a conflict seems highly probable.)

In teaching "Rita's Case," we have discovered that it is not easy for students to absorb the sequence of events, and so we have found that it helps to distribute a time-line of the major events in the case. We include this time-line here. (We place it on separate pages so instructors may photocopy it directly from this manual.):

RITA'S CASE — TIMELINE

12/71	Rita is born in New York City
3/72	Gladys becomes Rita's guardian
(no date)	Gladys, Rita, and Carlota move to Philadelphia
8/74	Gladys asks DPW for assistance with Rita while she recovers from surgery
8/74 - 6/76	Rita live in Catholic Home
6/76	Rita is placed in foster care in Germantown
(no date)	Gladys and Juan marry
2/77	Rita moves back into Gladys's home
6/77	Gladys again asks DPW for help; Rita moves back to Catholic Home
1/79	After report from psychology student, Catholic Home files CY47 form; Rita moves to foster care with the Biancos in Jenkintown; Gladys is not allowed to visit
3/79	At her social worker's suggestion, Gladys goes to Philadelphia Legal Aid (PLA) for help
5/10/79	PLA writes letter to DPW "terminating" DPW's custody of Rita
5/25/79	In response, DPW files a motion for temporary custody of Rita
6/8/79	PLA files 2 motions: a motion for Gladys to get visitation rights and a motion for payment for expert assistance in a psychological exam of Rita, to be conducted by St. Christophers.
6/11/79	Court appoints David Slade to represent Rita
3/80	St. Christophers arrives at preliminary findings favorable to Gladys
8/80	Slade voices concerns about St. Christophers findings, and requests that St. Christophers' inquiry include an evaluation of Gladys's home
Fall '80	Joan Kiladis joins Maynard in the case
1/29/81	Kiladis files petition for Gladys and Juan to adopt Rita
2/81	PLA files Gladys's New York guardianship records
2/82	Kiladis persuades Susan Goldman that DPW should dismiss its motions
4/82	At a hearing, DPW dismisses its motions, agrees to provide services to Gladys; Judge approves Gladys and Juan's motion to adopt Rita

<u>Note:</u> Professor Jack Sammons has produced a film of "Rita's Case" that some teachers may wish to show in conjunction with the reading. The film enacts a slightly different version of "Rita's Case" than ours, and teachers should review the film carefully to note the discrepancies. The film may be obtained through Professor Sammons at Mercer Law School, 1021 Georgia Avenue, Macon, Georgia, 31201-6709; telephone (478) 301-2323; email: jlsjr@aol.com.

Martha Minow, who supervised the preparation of "Rita's Case," has co-edited with Gary Bellow a collection of essays that includes one about the aftermath of the litigation. See "Rita's Case and Other Law Stories," in *Law Stories* 1 (Gary Bellow & Martha Minow, eds. 1996). As might be anticipated, Rita did not have an easy adolescence, although it is by no means clear that any other custodial options readily available would have been better.

An Alternative Introduction: The Film "Ethics in America: To Defend a Killer"

For those choosing not to begin the course with "Rita's Case," we suggest as an alternative a film produced by the Columbia School of Journalism. The film, "To Defend a Killer," is part of the "Ethics in America" series produced by Fred Friendly. It is a dramatic panel discussion moderated by Professor Charles Ogletree of Harvard Law School, and including distinguished lawyers, judges, journalists, academics, and other professionals who role-play and reflect on their responses as business executive John Barnes (enacted by Ogletree), who has just killed his lover, turns from one to another participant for advice. Students respond very strongly to the film, and it is a good momentum-generator at the beginning of the course. The film raises issues central to Chapters IV, V, and VI of the book -- and teachers who do not use it as an introduction to the course may wish to show it when it is time to teach these chapters.

One point of some interest to those using the film: at a dramatic moment in the film, a well-known Tennessee lawyer on the panel claims that violating the attorney-client privilege is a felony in Tennessee, a point that may confuse students.[6] The lawyer is wrong,

---

[6] The lawyer, James Neal, was the Chief Trial Counsel of the Watergate Special Prosecution Force in 1973 and 1974. Among his other high-profile cases, Mr. Neal subsequently represented Ford in the

although at the time the film was made, violating the privilege was a misdemeanor. Tennessee subsequently reclassified such a violation as an even more minor infraction. This is more than an inconsequential error. It appears at a point when Mr. Neal is arguing forcefully that "society" wishes attorneys to keep clients' secrets no matter what the cost to innocent third parties, and the fact that he misrepresents "society's" legal standard must be called to students' attention. Another possible point of confusion for students iis Justice Antonin Scalia's statement that a criminal defense client's confession to his lawyer about another, unrelated, past crime is not privileged. This is also incorrect: the client's confession about a completed act is protected by the privilege. Pedagogically, it can be useful to point out to students that even a Justice of the Supreme Court can get the law of privilege wrong -- teachers can remind students about this when teaching the crime-fraud exception to the attorney-client privilege.

Other videos and innovative teaching materials that may be suitable for introductory classes are identified in the annotated bibliography in 11 *Georgetown Journal of Legal Ethics* (1998).

Indiana Pinto case discussed in Chapter VII of this book.

CHAPTER I: THE CONCEPT OF A PROFESSION

We include this material at the beginning of the casebook because it raises questions that are fundamental to any course in the legal profession and its ethical regulation. What constitutes a profession and how distinctive is it from other occupations? What is the role of profit and public service? Some professors may find it easier to spark discussion if these materials come later in the course, once students have become comfortable talking, and more concrete issues have been addressed. These excerpts fit naturally into a discussion of the "crisis of professionalism" that has preoccupied many bar leaders over the past two decades. For those who feel that they don't have time to cover this material, it is possible to give students a brief exposure to contemporary debates by assigning only the ABA Commission's Report and the accompanying note material.

Chapter I's excerpts are designed to reflect varied ideological and interdisciplinary perspectives. The ABA Commission offers a traditional definition of professionalism, and Parsons provides its conventional sociological underpinnings. The Posner excerpt (as always, refreshing and iconoclastic) comes from a larger discussion of the similarities between the traditional legal profession and medieval trade guilds. Posner's main point – that the transition from guilds to a largely free market simultaneously helps consumers but makes life meaner and more miserable for producers – is an effective counterpoint to the ABA Report.

Issues surrounding the meaning of professionalism can usually generate good discussion. The quoted essay by Nelson and Trubek, as well as Rhode's excerpt, provide insight into the bar's recent angst. As both pieces note, the ABA's report is quite vague about the causes and consequences of the asserted decline of professionalism. What constitutes unprofessional conduct is equally unclear; the only examples that the Commission cites are tasteless advertising and litigation abuse. But if the ABA Commission is "unclear about what professionalism really means or why it is threatened by decline. . . [the Commission] has no shortage of recommendations as to what should be done . . . ."[1] The difficulty is that many of its prescriptions as well as

---

[1] Robert Nelson & David Trubek, "Arenas of Professionalism: The Professional Ideologies of Lawyers in Collective and Workplace Contexts," in *Lawyers' Ideals and Lawyers' Practice of the American*

diagnoses are somewhat superficial. Their "moralistic" tone and heavy emphasis on both individual altruism and law school education create a misleading impression. The implication is that our problems stem from simple greed or a lack of understanding about professional obligations, rather than from deeper "conflicts between idealized notions of desirable conduct and workplace pressures."[2]

One way to make this material seem more immediate and relevant to students is to ask what law schools could do to address the issue? Would they support professionalism programs along the lines that several institutions have adopted, which include speaker series and mentoring programs with lawyers in practice?

The readings in this chapter harmonize with a number of books and symposia on the profession. These include Deborah L. Rhode, *In the Interests of Justice* (2001); Richard Zitrin & Carol M. Langford, *The Moral Compass of the American Lawyer* (1999); Lincoln Caplan, *Skadden: Power, Money and the Rise of a Legal Empire* (1993); Anthony T. Kronman, *The Lost Lawyer: Failing Ideals of the Legal Profession* (1993); and the Professionalism Symposiums, in 52 S. Car. L. Rev. 443-758 (2001), and 54 S. Car. L. Rev. 869-1046 (2001).

Legal Profession (Robert Nelson, David Trubek & Rayman Solomon, eds. 1991).

[2] Id.

CHAPTER II: THE AMERICAN LEGAL PROFESSION

Historical Frameworks

We begin the chapter with materials on the historical development of the American legal profession. We expect that few teachers will spend significant class time on this material, but its few pages make useful background reading. The excerpt from Alexis de Tocqueville's *Democracy in America* is probably the most quoted analysis of the role of American lawyers ever written, and those who choose to omit this section may still wish to assign de Tocqueville. His central idea, that American lawyers play a mediating role between "the people" and the wealthy classes, and therefore constitute a natural "aristocracy," is justly famous. A contemporary effort to revive Tocqueville's theory, by the draftsman of the Model Rules, may be found in Geoffrey C. Hazard, Jr., "The Future of Legal Ethics," 100 *Yale L. J.* 1239 (1991). We have also included materials on bias in the profession because many students are unaware of this history and most are quite interested in its legacy.

Demographic Profiles

Demographic material can spark discussion along a variety of dimensions. On a descriptive level, it is worth exploring the forces that have encouraged professional growth, such as increases in government regulation, complex business organizations, and consumer demands in areas such as divorce. These explanations raise a further question for discussion: why have such forces in this country translated into a need for lawyers while in other nations, much of that need has been met by non-professionals with specialized training? Analysis of that issue may prompt speculation about future trends in the market for legal services. What are the implications of increasing scale, specialization, and stratification? As more attorneys and lay specialists practice in bureaucratic organizations with their own particular interests and norms (e.g., large law firms, in-house counsels' offices, government agencies), it may become more difficult to build consensus on unified professional standards.

The excerpt from "Personal Satisfaction in Professional Practice," newly added to this edition, offers an overview of the challenges in many legal practice settings. No issues are more central to students, and most have found it helpful to have a context for structured reflection. Inviting a practitioner who is especially thoughtful about these issues can also add a useful dimension to the discussion. In preparing a class on professionalism and the obstacles to fulfillment instructors may wish to consult the Symposium on Perspectives on Lawyer Happiness, 58 Syracuse L. Rev. 217 (2008) and the Symposium on Attorney Well-Being in Large Firms, 52 Vanderbilt L. Rev. 869 (1999). The featured article in the latter symposium, Patrick J. Schiltz's "On Being a Happy, Healthy, and Ethical Member of an Unhappy, Unhealthy, and Unethical Profession," 52 Vand. L. Rev. 871 (1999), is a well-known and highly provocative argument that the pressures of practice in large law firms are very likely to make young lawyers miserable and to erode their ethical sensibilities; for a sample of Schiltz's arguments, see the excerpt from his article we have included in Chapter VII, p. 447-48.

Students may also be interested in the "feminization" of the legal profession: why it has occurred and what consequences are likely to follow. Factors contributing to the trend are also explored in Chapter XVI on legal education, and in Chapter III's discussion of the regulation of the legal profession. Some of this material can be consolidated for a separate unit on gender, race, and ethnicity. The readings in Chapter II provide background on women's growing representation in the bar. Explanations for the increase include interrelated social, political, economic, and demographic forces such as: the growth of a women's movement; the passage of antidiscrimination legislation; increased expectations about standards of living; the rise in female labor force participation; the decline in birth rates; and the shortage of male professional school applicants during the Vietnam War. Questions for discussion might include: the effect of female entrants on professional status and pay scales; the underrepresentation of women in positions of greatest influence and economic reward; and the structural changes in legal practice that might be necessary to accommodate work and family values, such as alternative or reduced schedules. Professors who want to supplement casebook materials might look at Linda Hirshman's Get to Work,, the ABA Commission on Women in the Profession's *Visible Invisibility: Women of Color in Law Firms* (2006), or the National Association of Women Lawyers, Actions for Advancing Women into Law Firm Leadership (2008). Hirshman's advice includes "Have a baby, just don't have two" (p. 62); NAWL's recommendations include refining evaluation and compensation systems, providing training in professional development, and tracking gender equity.

Problems surrounding minority recruitment and advancement are an important topic for discussion. Further materials appear in the chapters on admission and on legal education and these could also be consolidated for discussion. Specific topics for exploration can include affirmative action, recruitment, and informal patterns of segregation that arise both in law schools and in legal practice. The highly-publicized case of Lawrence Mungen can form a centerpiece for the discussion; it is particularly useful to discuss Lichtenberg's distinction between "racism in the head" and "racism in the world".

Aaron Charney's highly publicized lawsuit against Sullivan and Cromwell can offer a similarly rich case study concerning sexual orientation. A good account of the dispute is Robert Kolker's "The Gray Flannel Suit," *New York Magazine*, February 26, 2007. Charney cites evidence of what he took to be homophobic comments, and retaliation for making a discrimination complaint. In defense of the firm's reputation, one partner felt that the lawyer who had made the offensive remarks was "equal opportunity rude and nasty." Eleven openly gay partners issued a public statement rejecting any suggestion that the firm fosters a hostile environment. Charney's response was that "It's totally unclear to me how somebody who has never met me could suggest that because we sit in the same building and he's in an environment that he's happy in, that that is any way reflective of what's happening in my environment." This case, like the one discussed in *The Good Black*, raise issues not just about diversity, but also about how legal employers should build a culture of respect and professional opportunities for all its junior attorneys. Students can also consider how they might contribute to this objective, through organizations such as Building a Better Legal Profession.

For professors who wish to include class exercises on these topics, we include several possibilities below.

CLASSROOM EXERCISES

Legal Workplace Simulation

To explore diversity-related issues, the class could break into subgroups representing different employment organizations (such as a large law firm, a small firm, an in-house counsel department, an understaffed/ legal service office) and different roles within those organizations (a conservative managing partner, a gay attorney who has not disclosed his sexual orientation, a junior partner who has decided not to have children, etc.). Each group of students should attempt to formulate policies on the following issues:

Affirmative Action

Whom should the policy cover? Should efforts be limited to recruitment or should any preferential treatment be given in hiring and promotion? Should the organization establish goals and timetables? How should they be implemented?

Alternative Work Schedules and Family Policies

Who should be able to take part-time status or work an alternative schedule? For example, should flexible scheduling options cover non-lawyer staff? Should only parents with small children be eligible, or should equivalent arrangements be available for individuals who wish to devote more time to handling pro bono cases or writing poetry? Should the policy include any time limits? What effect should part-time status have on compensation, bonuses, and consideration for partner? Who should absorb additional overhead costs? How will part-time status affect travel assignments? Should full-time attorneys be able to opt out of travel or late hours because of family obligations? If so, how will those needs be covered?

Diversity and Quality of Life Issues

What other steps should employers take to address diversity and quality of life issues? How should billable hour requirements and compensation policies be established? What recruitment, retention, mentoring, and training policies would you support?

Bias in the Workplace

Alternatively, students should take the test on implicit racial bias at www.implicit.harvard.edu or www.tolerance.org, and then break into small groups. Each group should use a flip chart to make a visual image of their experience at law school. The class should reconvene as a whole and each group should explain their group portrait. Issues to consider include:

- How does it feel to be a member of this group at your law

school?

- What is the experience of your group in the classroom, and in relationships with faculty, administrators, and other students?

- How do law school practices and policies affect the success of your group?[1]

Sex Discrimination Lawsuit

The first sex discrimination case to go to trial against a law firm, Ezold v. Wolf, Block, Schor, and Solis-Cohen, could provide the vehicle for various role simulations. A case study of the litigation appears in Deborah L. Rhode, "What's Sex Got to Do With It," in Legal Ethics: Law Stories (Deborah L. Rhode & David Luban, eds. Foundation Press, 2006). Students could be assigned the role of lawyers for the plaintiff or the law firm, or lawyers on the firm management committee determining whether to offer a settlement or modify their evaluation and promotion procedures.

---

[1] This exercise is adapted from a much more elaborate exercise designed by the Kaleel Jamison Consulting Group, Troy, New York.

CHAPTER III: PROFESSIONAL AUTONOMY

The material in this chapter raises questions that are central to any analysis of professional regulation:

1) What is the appropriate role of professional associations?

2) What are the functions of professional codes?

3) What degree of autonomy should the profession exercise in regulating its membership?

In addition, the chapter discusses a rule-based question that is becoming increasingly central to ethics debates as legal practice goes multi-state and multi-national – the choice-of-law issues involved in determining which jurisdiction's ethics rules apply.

Doing It Quickly

For instructors who do not wish to spend much time on this chapter, we suggest the following as a minimal way to cover the crucial material.

First, we would assign the ABA's 1906 Report (pp. 114-16) justifying the writing of a code of professional ethics. It is worth dwelling on the Report's rhetoric: e.g. the code of ethics as "a beacon light on the mountain of high resolve to lead the young practitioner safely through the snares and pitfalls of his early practice up to and along the straight and narrow path of high and honorable professional achievement." It is also worth noting that while President Roosevelt had admonished the ABA about the public problem of hardball lawyering on behalf of well-heeled clients, the ABA's report criticizes only "the shyster, the barratrously inclined, the ambulance chaser, the member of the Bar with a system of runners, [who] pursue their nefarious methods with no check save the rope of sand of moral suasion . . ." – in other words, lawyers representing clients of limited means.

Second, we would include an overview of the Model Rules – discussing with students the way the Rules classifies topics in its eight principal sections, coupled with a brief discussion of its regulatory philosophy as described in the preamble and scope sections.

Third, if time permits, we would discuss the jurisdiction and choice-of-law materials. Problems 2 and 3 will probably take at least half-an-hour to do properly. Because they involve detail-work with the difficult rule 8.5, students should be asked in advance to prepare answers to the questions these problems pose. Teachers may wish to use only one of these problems.

Teachers may wish to combine some of the materials from this chapter with additional materials on the disciplinary process from Chapter XV into a single unit on professional self-regulation and discipline. These materials might include Section C on disciplinary sanctions, perhaps combined with section D on mental health and substance abuse.

***

The chapter begins by placing issues of professional regulation in historical perspective. Teachers who are pressed for time may wish to omit this section or to summarize some key points in a lecture. The selections from Hurst and Auerbach discuss the evolution of the American Bar Association from a small, homogeneous, elitist organization into the major representative of the profession as a whole. This development suggests questions along several lines. What social, economic, and cultural forces contributed to the ABA's expansion? Relevant factors for analysis might include considerations that social historians have lumped under the label "status anxiety." In this instance, such considerations would include elite attorneys' concerns about how unrestricted entry and competitive behavior by religious and ethnic minorities might affect the profession's public image. So too, the widespread nativism of the 1920s and the economic depression of the 1930s fueled bar leaders' desire for a strong professional association that could exercise greater power over competition, admission, and discipline.

Lawyers, it should be pointed out, were not unique in this respect. The late nineteenth and early twentieth centuries witnessed a rapid growth of vocational organizations committed to improving their members' social and economic status. The range of these groups is noted briefly in the section on lay competition and unauthorized practice; they included awning installers, house painters, frog dealers, and dancing school instructors.[1] One issue worth pursuing in some depth is how bar organizations compare to other trade groups.

Certain obvious distinctions involve the exercise of political power. Unlike other vocational groups, the ABA does not offer endorsements or financial contributions to political candidates. Moreover, as the Hurst excerpt reflects, the bar has long engaged in law reform activities that do not serve in any direct way to further the socio-economic interests of its membership.

Yet by the same token, the ABA and its state analogues have also pursued a variety of regulatory objectives that clearly elevate the concerns of attorneys and sometimes their major clients over those of the general public.

As other commentators have also noted, ABA membership reflects a skewed segment of the profession: it overrepresents lawyers from large private firms and underrepresents groups such as solo practitioners, racial minorities, academics, and public interest lawyers. Given this pattern, it is appropriate to ask what sort of role the ABA should play in speaking for lawyers as a group.

A related, and still more critical question, is what role the organized bar should have in formulating policy for the profession. Chapter III raises that question in the context of ethical codes. Subsequent chapters, particularly Chapter XII on market regulation and Chapter XV on discipline, will return to these issues in the context of specific substantive policies.

The readings on bar ethical codes again start offering a historical context. The 1906 ABA Report is an effective teaching tool because it acknowledges so explicitly the profession's status concerns. A fruitful question to explore in class is how central these status issues remain. The organized bar's longstanding resistance to many forms of advertising, solicitation, and non-lawyer competition and ownership may be some indication of ongoing concerns in this area. Similarly, recent

---

[1] Jethro Lieberman, *The Tyranny of the Experts: How Professionals are Doing in the Open Society*, 14-17 (1980).

surveys have suggested that lawyers still believe that the most important issue facing the profession is their public standing.

The Luban/Millemann excerpt criticizes the evolution of the ethics codes away from incorporating moral standards. It also highlights a crucial fact: that ethics codes play only a modest role in the total legal regulation of lawyer behavior. The excerpt's example of lawyers' duties to represent unpopular clients can serve as a focal-point for discussion.

Exploration of the profession's image-related concerns provides a good transition into Judith Lichtenberg's analysis of professional codes. One way to begin discussion is to ask whether professional codes have served more to express or limit self-interest. For example, L. Ray Patterson has argued that the "ultimate function of a code of legal ethics is to keep within reasonable bounds the law of self-interest that operates at all times and in all places."[2] By contrast, William Moore has maintained that professional codes may sometimes serve as "window dressing, more designed to give false comfort to the laity than guide the practitioner."[3] Professors interested in other critiques of such codes, building on critical legal theory, might look at Richard Abel's article in a 1981 symposium on the Model Rules.[4]

Such perspectives contrast well with traditional idealized

---

[2] L. Ray Patterson, "The Function of a Code of Legal Ethics," 35 *U. of Miami L. Rev.* 695, 723 (1981).

[3] William Moore, *The Professions: Roles and Rules* 119 (1970).

[4] Richard Abel, "Why Does the ABA Promulgate Ethical Rules?," 59 *Texas L. Rev.* 639 (1981).

accounts of the potential value of professional ethics. Some contemporary commentators, including the authors of this casebook, believe that the bar's affirmation of shared values may play a constructive role in socializing new practitioners and in shaping practice norms. However, it is not self-evident that current regulatory codes are the best vehicle for this collective expression. Further elaborations of this point appear in articles by Murray Schwartz and Geoffrey Hazard.[5]

The costs of allowing the bar full regulatory independence are set forth in the Rhode excerpt. A useful class exercise is to ask whether society would be well served by doctors regulating doctors or auto mechanics regulating auto mechanics, without some external checks. The difference, of course, is that the dangers of government oversight are much greater with lawyers than with other professionals. The kind of show trials available in countries without an independent legal profession do not provide attractive models for export. It is, however, important to point out that full independence and totalitarian control are not the only options. Many Anglo European countries are moving toward "co-regulatory" approaches that draw on both professional organizations and independent consumer regulatory structures. An interesting issue for class discussion would be how to build a political constituency in support of such alternatives, given the diffuse public support that they are likely to command and the strong professional opposition that they would doubtless provoke.

Professional Regulation and Choice of Law

Problems 2 and 3 highlight the complexities and ambiguities surrounding jurisdiction and choice of law in legal ethics contexts. They raises several important pedagogical points. The first is that major differences between various jurisdictions' ethics rules can create significant problems for lawyers. The second is the simple but often-forgotten point that it *is* the different jurisdictions' rules, not the ABA Model Rules, that matter in practice. The third is a more subtle point,

---

[5] Murray L. Schwartz, "The Death and Regeneration of Ethics," 1981 *A.B.F. Res. J.* 953; Geoffrey C. Hazard, Jr., "Legal Rules and Professional Aspirations," 30 *Clev. St. L. Rev.* 521 (1981).

but a very important one: in many contexts no authoritative answer exists to a basic question: "which jurisdiction's ethics rules govern me in this case?"

Problem 2:

This problem is an exercise in using Model Rule 8.5, on jurisdiction and choice of law.

a) This problem is modeled on some of the facts of *In re* Hager, 812 A.2d 904 (D.C. 2002), and the unpublished New Jersey opinion *In the Matter of* Karel L. Zaruba, Docket No. 03-98, at 4. These cases are discussed in the text, page 682, Question 3.

The question raised by this part of the problem is quite straightforward: do disciplinary authorities in State X have long-arm jurisdiction over conduct by a lawyer licensed only in another state? The applicable rule is 8.5(a), which provides jurisdiction over the conduct of an out-of-state lawyer "if the lawyer provides or offers to provide any legal services in this jurisdiction." Given that (1) Ross is licensed only in State Y, (2) the two attorneys negotiated the settlement in State Y, and (3) the settlement affected only the interests of clients in State Y, there appears to be no basis for State X to exert jurisdiction over Ross's conduct. The problem also asks whether it would make a difference if the lawyers had negotiated the settlement in State X. This is a bit more complicated. One possible answer is that simply negotiating the settlement in the territory of State X is not providing legal services in State X (because the client is not in X), and so the outcome is the same: no jurisdiction. However, in August 2002, the ABA House of Delegates amended Model Rule 8.5(b)(2), and the amended version stipulates that for non-litigation conduct, the rules that apply are those "of the jurisdiction in which the lawyer's conduct occurred..." – a territorial test. A lawyer trying to find a consistent reading of parts (a) and (b) of Rule 8.5 might reason that if the rules to be applied for conduct that took place in State X are those of that state, then X ought to be able to exert jurisdiction. In other words, why use a territorial test for choice of law but not for jurisdiction? Despite this argument, we find the original answer – no jurisdiction in this matter – more plausible.

b) Part (b) again raises a troubling question of long-arm disciplinary jurisdiction. The problem stipulates that unethical conduct by a lawyer

31

constitutes fraud in a jurisdiction where the lawyer does not live and is not licensed (State Z), and where none of the lawyer's clients lives. A straightforward reading of Model Rule 8.5(a) would hold that State Z cannot exercise long-arm jurisdiction over Mark's conduct despite the fact that it amounts to fraud in Z.

The two halves of this problem raise the basic policy question of how jurisdiction connects with interests. In part (a), it is possible that State X can exert jurisdiction over Ross even though Ross's conduct affected no interests in X; while in part (b), State Z cannot exert jurisdiction even though Ross's conduct harms interests in Z. This is one of the well-recognized drawbacks to a purely territorial approach to jurisdiction.

Problem 3:

The question of which state's rules of professional conduct govern a lawyer – the choice-of-law question – differs from the question of which state or states may exert jurisdiction over that lawyer's conduct. Problem 2 addressed the latter question; the current problem raises the choice-of-law issue. This is non-litigation conduct, and so the governing rule is 8.5(b)(2). Under the former (pre-2002) version of 8.5(b)(2), the rules governing the conduct of a lawyer licensed in multiple jurisdictions would be those of the jurisdiction in which the lawyer primarily practices (unless the predominant effect of the conduct occurred in another jurisdiction). The August 2002 revision switched to a territorial test: the rules that govern are those of the jurisdiction in which the conduct occurs (again, unless the predominant effect of the conduct occurs in another jurisdiction). Here, the territorial test yields the result that New York's rules should apply. But on the facts of this problem, the predominant effect of the conduct is plainly not in New York: the conduct has no direct effects whatever in New York. But where is the predominant effect? It seems as though the conduct has effects in both Missouri and New Jersey. If the lawyer allows the deal to proceed, New Jersey purchasers will suffer financial losses, which makes it seem as though the predominant effect of the conduct is in New Jersey. That would imply that New Jersey's mandatory-disclosure rule applies, and so the lawyer is subject to discipline for not disclosing. On the other hand, if the lawyer discloses, the Missouri client may well suffer financial losses, in which case one might argue that the predominant effect of the conduct is in Missouri. But in that case, Missouri's no-disclosure rule applies, and the lawyer is subject to discipline. Clearly, this is a lose-lose situation for the lawyer: no matter what he or she does, the lawyer has violated an applicable rule of conduct. If, on the other hand, one concludes that neither the Missouri nor New Jersey effects predominate over the other – the lawyer's conduct, whatever it is, will have effects in both states – we are back to the territorial test, and New York's rule applies. This seems like the most workable answer, even though the result is unusual: the lawyer's conduct is regulated by the rules of a state that has no connection with the case other than the fact that a meeting was held in that state. This problem may be used to emphasize to students the trade-offs involved in the ABA's territorial approach: a territorial rule is relatively easy to understand and administer, but when the conduct has little to do with the state it occurs in, the simplicity of the rule carries costs in how sensible the outcome is.

CHAPTER IV: THE ADVOCATE'S ROLE IN AN ADVERSARY SYSTEM

This chapter raises fundamental questions about what has sometimes been called "the lawyer's amoral role" and its grounding in the adversary system. Lawyers sometimes represent a client whose goals or conduct they find distasteful.. Understanding the ethical arguments on behalf of (or against) this role is, in our view, one of the primary aims of a professional responsibility course. In line with our overall approach, the materials that follow aim to raise these arguments in the context of particular cases.

Doing It Quickly

For teachers who do not wish to spend much time on these issues, we suggest the following as the minimum material to assign: sections A - D.2, including Problems 1 and 2; section E.1, including Problem 4; and then one of either the material on discovery abuse, including *Qualcomm*, or the material on civility, including *Lee v. American Eagle Airlines*. This subset of the materials totals fewer than 50 pages. It combines criticisms of the amoral ethical role, various efforts to justify that role, the best-known defense of the adversary system (Fuller and Randall), a critique of that defense, and some black-letter law to reassure the less theoretically-minded students that the issues do have direct doctrinal counterparts. With a bit of squeezing, this minimum set of materials can be covered in a single two-hour class, although three class hours is better.

Much of the chapter examines one conception of how lawyers should live their professional lives. This is the familiar model of "neutral partisanship," sometimes called "zealous advocacy," and less flatteringly the "hired gun" model. Neutral partisanship combines a demand that attorneys advance their clients' interests within the bounds of the law with an insistence that lawyers should be morally neutral toward their clients' ends. The neutral partisanship conception insists that lawyers are morally unaccountable for the means used and ends achieved in their representation. This conception was first analyzed in the late 1970s and early 1980s by commentators such as Richard Wasserstrom, Murray Schwartz, William Simon, Gerald Postema, David Luban, and Deborah Rhode; we begin with Simon's exposition of neutral partisanship. Later in the chapter we consider alternatives to neutral partisanship. To illustrate what it might mean for lawyers to abandon neutrality, we present a case-study of an internal debate within Cravath, Swaine and Moore over whether it would be immoral to represent a Swiss bank alleged to have laundered Nazi gold during World War II. And to illustrate the limits on lawyer partisanship, we have added materials on when lawyers may be criminally liable for assisting clients in activities of doubtful legality.

In addition to raising fundamental ethical questions, the chapter also considers issues concerning adversarial procedures. The most common attempts to explain the morality of legal practice in our society point to the central role of the adversary system and the requirements that it imposes. For this reason, we include both American and comparative materials that permit assessment of adversarial processes.

Finally, we include readings that explore characteristic adversarial abuses and current attempts to control them. The central topics are F.R.C.P. Rule 11, discovery abuse, and civility.

A. The "Neutral Partisanship" Conception of the Lawyer's Role

Neutral partisanship offers a tidy and compelling framework for legal ethics, but neither life nor law is quite so tidy. Two threshold questions, then, are to what extent the Model Rules embodies neutral partisanship and to what extent lawyers adopt that conception of their role.[1]

---

[1] Ted Schneyer has argued forcefully that the Code and Model Rules are only partly committed to neutral partisanship. Ted Schneyer, "Moral Philosophy's Standard Misconception of Legal Ethics," 1984 *Wisc. L. Rev.* 1529 (1984). See in addition the exchange in M. B. E. Smith, "Should Lawyers Listen to Philosophers About Legal Ethics?," 9 *Law and Philosophy* 67 (1991), David Luban, "Smith Against the Ethicists," 9 *Law and Philosophy* 417 (1990-91), and M. B. E. Smith,

Problem 1 provides an introduction to the topic that is interesting primarily because, unusually, the official reaction of the bar (evidenced in Formal Opinion 92-368) is to reject zealous advocacy. Lawyers simply have a gut reaction that peeking at the adversary's documents is unfair, and that you'd better not do it because what goes around comes around. Freedman's forceful reply clearly has the better of the argument – but the Committee's conclusion seems more palatable to many, which exposes a weakness in neutral partisanship. Andrew Perlman, in the article cited in note 8, p. 147, proposes that if a lawyer discovers the mistake before the opposing counsel has read the document, that counsel must not read it and must comply with the lawyer's instructions about the document. If an attorney knows from examination of the document that it contains privileged information, the attorney should stop reading it and has discretion whether to notify the sender. In Perlman's view, discretion is appropriate because the competing values are fairly evenly balanced.

An interesting variation on this issue is the subject of Professional Ethics Committee of the Florida Bar, Opinion 07-1 (2007). There, a wife who gave her divorce attorney documents that the client either removed from the husband's office, printed from the husband's computor, or accessed on her own computer with the husband's password. The Committee concluded that the material could not be retained or reviewed or used without disclosure, and that if the client did not consent, the attorney must withdraw from representation. The Commitee also suggested advising the client that she may have committed a criminal act, and should seek guidance from a criminal defense attorney.

New to this edition of the book is the discussion of the metadata issue on pages 147-48. A useful hypothetical for raising the issue in acute form is this: suppose that a lawyer exposes and reads the metadata on settlement documents sent by an adversary, and discovers comments that reveal the adversary's settlement limits. It would be very difficult not to use this information in settlement negotiations. For those who believe that it is unethical to use information that was plainly supposed to be confidential, is the conclusion that the lawyer must not even read the metadata? Or, as Freedman suggests in the "errant fax" problem, that he or she must read the metadata? That a law firm with a capable IT department

---

"Reply to David Luban," 10 *Law and Philosophy* 427 (1991).

should routinely expose metadata on all pertinent documents? Because of the danger of inadvertent disclosure of metadata, many lawyers now routinely convert all Word documents to PDFs before sending them to adversaries. However, technologies may soon exist that permit the retrieval of metadata even from PDFs.

Problem 2 is another attempt to display the uncomfortable implications of neutral partisanship. A. H. Robins's lawyers' "dirty questions" (part (a)) included asking plaintiffs how often they engage in anal sex, whether they wipe from front to back or back to front when they go to the toilet, and what material the crotch of their panty-hose is made of. (It was this last question that provoked one plaintiff to reply, "I'll answer that, but it sounds like an obscene phone call.") The case in part (b) was a takeover fight between Conoco and Seagram's (whose board chairman, Edgar Bronfman, headed the world Zionist organization); the tactic described in the problem was originated by Conoco's counsel, the legendary mergers and acquisitions lawyer Joseph Flom.

Most students are attracted to the neutral partisanship conception of the lawyer's role, and many believe strongly that the adversary system requires tough, competitive advocacy from both sides. What makes the questions in Problem 2 uncomfortable for these students is that defense by intimidation strikes many as going beyond the rules of fair play. Professors can ask students whether the adversary system really requires lawyers to try to coerce the other side into giving up without a fight. The problem is useful for another reason as well: often, lawyers defend the adversary system by arguing that partisan advocacy is the best way to ensure that all sides of a dispute get heard. The first three examples in this problem, however, consist of tactics designed to drive one side out of the case rather than to maximize all sides' input into it.

Another tactic that could spark heated class discussion is the decision of the Boston Catholic Archdiocese or its lawyers to subpoena the psychiatric records of opponents suing for sex abuse by clergy. In some instances, the psychiatrists had been hired by the Archdiocese to provide treatment for the abuse survivors. The tactic did not violate any ethical rules because the psychotherapist privilege is waived when a plaintiff claims damages for emotional trauma. But according to Steven Lubet in the Importance of Being Honest: How Lying, Secrecy, and Hypocrisy Collide With Truth in Law (NYU Press,

2008), the strategy was a "moral disaster" (p. 21). A coalition of psychotherapists and victims' rights activists denounced the "revictimization" of survivors, which was inconsistent with the Archdiocese's professed commitment to justice and healing. In response, a spokesperson for Church blamed their counsel: "It's a very tragic set of circumstances, but when you get to the litigation stage, there are certain things lawyers insist on doing to protect their clients."Id. Lubet blamed the client for wanting to "raise the flag of reconciliation while instructing counsel to scorch the earth." Id., at 22. Students can debate whether there is plenty of blame to go around.

B. Neutral Partisanship and Role Morality;
and
C. The Justification of Neutral Partisanship

In this edition, we have shortened the philosophical discussion of role morality. The only difficult part of this discussion is the material from Arthur Applbaum's book *Ethics for Adversaries* on page 153. Applbaum's point is that it is very easy to confuse the first argument in each pair (which, he claims, is true but doesn't justify much) with the similar-sounding second argument (which justifies hardball behavior but isn't obviously true). It is worth going through a couple of Applbaum's pairs to see what he means. Thus, it is probably often true that adversaries in contentious negotiations expect to be lied to. But expecting to be lied to isn't the same as consenting to be lied to, so the common argument that it's okay to lie because the other side expects it (i.e., consents to it) simply doesn't work. It is probably true that the rules of litigation permit hardball tactics (for example, the "dirty questions" in Problem 2(a)); and it is true that the rules are the same for both sides. But it doesn't follow that fair play morally permits hardball tactics. The rules themselves might be morally unjustifiable. The fact that both sides play under the same unacceptable rules is irrelevant. Applbaum's critique is extremely valuable, because the six pairs of arguments he canvasses are the ones that defenders of adversarial professional morality always invoke – and none of them are sound. But, if Applbaum is right, that still leaves the question of what the alternative is. For a striking exploration of this point through the example of Charles–Henri Sanson, the public executioner during the French Revolution, *see* Arthur Isak Applbaum, "Professional Detachment: The Executioner of Paris," 109 *Harv. L. Rev.* 958 (1995), *reprinted in* Applbaum, at 17–42

D. The Adversary System

The section on the adversary system begins by looking at the two principal justifications of adversarial procedure: that it is the best way to get at the truth, and that it is the best way to protect individual rights. Fuller and Randall's defense of the adversary system as a finder of truth is justly famous, and quite subtle. Luban's critique, on the other hand, is quite blunt. The trickiest part of this debate is raised in Question 1. Fuller and Randall argue that the adversary system is superior to the inquisitorial system because the inquisitorial judge has too much invested in sticking to his or her original theory of the case and isn't sufficiently open-minded. But Fuller and Randall also argue that adversarial advocacy goes too far when it "muddies the headwaters of decision." The problem is that many lawyer's tactics in the adversary system are themselves attempts to keep information out of the hearing, and that "muddies the headwaters of decision." Thus, one implication of the Fuller/Randall defense of the adversary system is that there must be strict limits to advocacy. For example, in his famous essay "The Adversary System," Fuller argues that a criminal defense lawyer "may not, to free his client, cast suspicion on innocent persons."[2] Of course, this is completely contrary to the views of virtually every criminal defense lawyer. (We discuss this question in the chapter on confidentiality.)

This section includes some comparative materials on an "inquisitorial" system, that of Germany. Our conviction is that discussion of adversarial premises should be informed by some idea of the alternatives. Both Langbein's descriptions of German civil procedure and Bedford's journalistic account of a German criminal trial offer attractive portraits, ones that may dispel some of the stereotypes that "inquisitorial" procedures often evoke. Although both readings are decades old, they are not out of date. Given that a surprising number of students often jump to the conclusion that the German system is preferable to our own, the discussion questions draw attention to certain disadvantages of inquisitorial practice. One of the key points is that the German "conference" method of civil procedure, which involves long interludes between meetings, makes it virtually impossible to

---

[2] Fuller, "The Adversary System," in *Talks on American Law* 30 (Harold J. Berman ed. 1961), at 38.

impanel a jury. The German system may gain in efficiency and truth-finding, but it loses in popular control. The difference in expert witness practice illustrates this graphically: the German expert witness has no incentive to massage the truth, but parties risk drawing an unfavorable expert, with little recourse for finding one more favorable to their own position. The other main objection to the German procedure is a practical, financial one: an "inquisitorial" system needs a much larger judiciary than Americans are used to, and it seems doubtful that Americans would be willing to hire ten times as many judges as we now have. Question 2 makes this point.

Problem 3 returns to "Rita's Case," and teachers should draw two points from it: first, that to some degree the difference between Maynard and Kiladis is the difference between Neutral Partisanship and its alternatives; second, that Rita's case illustrates much that is problematic about the adversary system.

E. Alternatives to Neutral Partisanship

The section on alternatives begins with a brief overview of several prominent alternatives to neutral partisanship that have appeared in scholarship on legal ethics. Professors pressed for time may prefer to condense or omit this discussion and turn directly to Problems 4 and 5.

Problem 4. This problem is modeled on the case of Cravath's representation of Credit Suisse, discussed in the materials immediately following the problem. The legal background and facts about the Rwandan genocide are accurate. Although Mr. M. is imaginary, he is a composite of real figures, notably former Rwandan Prime Minister Jean Kambanda, who was sentenced to life in prison for genocide and crimes against humanity, and other figures such as Léon Mugesera who made radio speeches inciting genocide. Unhappily, the reference to Tutsis as "cockroaches" is not imaginary: it was a common slur among the Hutu death squads. The only imaginary part of the problem is Mr. M.'s looting of Rwandese government funds.

The Cravath debate about representing Crédit Suisse was widely reported in the press. Ironically, a less well-known case -- highly relevant to Problem 4 – also involved Cravath, Swaine and Moore's representation of an alleged human rights violator. In the early 1990s, Royal Dutch Petroleum (the owner of Shell Oil) engaged in oil exploration in Nigeria, and a vigorous local opposition movement arose among the Ogoni people, whose lands were threatened. Allegedly at the behest of Shell Nigeria, the Nigerian government sent police and soldiers to suppress the opposition movement, and in 1995, despite pleas from around the world, the Nigerian government hanged opposition leader Ken Saro-Wiwa as well as other Ogoni activists. Surviving victims joined Wiwa's family in an Alien Tort claim filed in New York, alleging that Royal Dutch Petroleum had lobbied the Nigerian government to torture and murder the Ogoni activists. See *Wiwa v. Royal Dutch Petroleum*, 226 F.3d 88 (2nd Cir. 2000).

Royal Dutch Petroleum retained Cravath. The firm drew the wrath of human rights lawyers by petitioning the U.S. Supreme Court to grant certiorari, arguing that the Alien Tort Claims Act was unconstitutional. (The Court denied cert, and in *Sosa v. Alvarez-Machain*, 542 U.S. 692 (2004), rejected the legal theory employed in the *Wiwa* cert petition.) The *Wiwa* case raises the issue of zealous advocacy and moral neutrality in stark terms: human rights advocates were angered that Cravath would, on behalf of one client, attempt to eviscerate the most important law for litigating human rights cases in U.S. courts. Students can consider whether Cravath associates should have written another letter to the partners about the *Wiwa* representation.

2. The Limits of Partisanship

This section explores the issue of the limits of partisanship by examining lawyer criminal liability for efforts on behalf of clients. The question, in a phrase used by several courts, is when a criminal lawyer crosses the line to become a lawyer-criminal. We believe that this is an important but often neglected topic. Many lawyers and law students believe, perhaps unconsciously, in a kind of "advocate's immunity": steps taken to further client interests are often assumed not to implicate the lawyer. As a matter of law, this is entirely false: a lawyer who aids a client crime is an accomplice. The federal mail fraud and wire fraud statutes criminalize any "scheme or artifice to defraud" utilizing the mails, private couriers like Federal Express, the telephone, or the Internet. Obviously, virtually anything a lawyer does will use one of these channels of communication, and thus the potential for mail or wire fraud liability for lawyers who further a client's frauds is vast.

As a matter of prosecutorial practice, however, the "advocate's immunity" has some basis: federal prosecutors typically go after lawyers only when they are convinced that the lawyers are knowingly assisting criminal activities.

Problem 5. For the reason just indicated – prosecutors don't typically indict lawyers unless they are active participants in crime – the prosecution of tobacco company lawyers is almost unthinkable. Students may be outraged at the suggestion that tobacco company lawyers committed federal crimes. The primary task for the professor is not to disagree with their outrage, but to get students to articulate why the tobacco case differs from *Cueto* and the Cali cartel cases. The problem notes that the Justice Department filed civil RICO charges against the tobacco industry, and the elements of civil RICO and criminal RICO are essentially identical. In 2006, Judge Gladys Kessler found that "there is overwhelming evidence to support most of the Government's allegations," *U.S. v. Philip Morris et al.*, 449 F.Supp.2d 1, 27 (D.D.C. 2006). Her opinion ran to more than 1,500 pages, and held the defendants liable for civil RICO. Thus, if prosecutors wished they could seek indictments of tobacco companies for RICO violations using the same theory as the civil RICO suit. And, if the tobacco industry could be indicted, so could the lawyers who (as evidence summarized in the problem suggests) were participants rather than mere agents in formulating the industry's strategy. In many cases, statutes of limitation would foreclose prosecuting lawyers who orchestrated tobacco industry frauds decades ago. But, if some lawyers and law firms made more recent conscious decisions to continue the frauds, statutes of limitations may not eliminate all potential criminal liability. That liability extends not only to individual lawyers but also to law firms under federal respondeat superior principles (under which an employee's crime within the actual or apparent scope of the employee's duties can be charged to the employer).

U.S. v. Cueto. This is quite an alarming case. Cueto goes to prison for 7 years for filing legal motions, conducting cross-examinations, and complaining to the authorities about an undercover agent who is soliciting bribes from Cueto's client to entrap him. Obviously, the prosecutor, jury, and appellate court believe that Cueto was as much a mobster as a lawyer – but, as the court notes in footnote 10, p. 192, this was not the theory behind the government's case. Instead, the theory was that litigating on behalf of a mobster, knowing that he is a mobster, is obstruction of justice. Perhaps the result is a just one, but if so the court has not articulated a rationale for it that wouldn't apply equally well to virtually any lawyer trying to use procedural means to keep an investigation off his or her client's back.

Amiel Cueto – quite a flamboyant character – was released from prison in 2004 after serving his sentence. Cueto insisted that he would fight to get his conviction overturned and his law license back. A former prosecutor and personal injury lawyer, Cueto was in the news as recently as 2007 because of defamation suits against journalists.

The prosecutions of the Cali cartel lawyers, **Question 3**, page 195, is along the lines of *Cueto*, except that the lawyers did more problematic things on behalf of their clients than Cueto did on behalf of Venezia. The most damning tactic was that they approached imprisoned cartel employees and got them to execute false affidavits stating that they did not know Miguel Rodriguez-Orojuela. However, they never filed the affidavits. For further factual details, see the chapter on the Cali lawyers in James Kelly, *Lawyers Crossing Lines* (2001).

The Lynne Stewart case. This case raises the question of how far lawyers can go on behalf of their clients in a particularly compelling context: the War on Terror. More specifically, the issue is how far lawyers for terrorists can go without themselves attracting criminal liability for providing "material support" to terrorism. The material support statutes, 18 U.S.C. §§2339A-C, were originally enacted under the Clinton Administration's Antiterrorism and Effective Death Penalty Act (AEDPA) of 1996, then beefed up by the USA PATRIOT Act.

Students are likely to divide over the Lynne Stewart case. Stewart, as the materials indicate, is a sympathetic defendant, especially to left-leaning students; but most students are likely to believe that Stewart crossed an important line when she decided to hold a press conference announcing that the Sheik no longer supported a cease-fire (a statement that clearly seems to encourage acts of terrorism by his followers). The excerpt from Abbe Smith's thoughtful article on Lynne Stewart can help focus the discussion. Smith seems to agree that Stewart stepped over a line, but argues that good, zealous defense lawyers are temperamentally inclined to defy government efforts to silence them or their clients, and thus that the kind of defense lawyer that ethical rules encourage is precisely the kind of lawyer most likely to do what Stewart did. Steven Lubet, in his recent book, *The Importance of Being Honest,* is even more critical of Stewart.

As this book goes to press, Stewart's case remains under appeal. Before teaching it, professors should check Stewart's website (www.lynnestewart.org) for updates.

The USA PATRIOT Act amended the material support statute after Lynne Stewart's conduct. Crucially, the amendment adds the provision of "expert advice and assistance" as a form of material support for terrorism. This amendment raises the question of whether any form of legal advocacy on behalf of designated terrorists counts as material support and could lead to criminal liability for lawyers. Presumably, courtroom advocacy is immune from prosecution. But what about other forms of legal representation, such as advising designated FTOs in their activities? *Cueto* suggests that even ordinarily-protected lawyer activities can be found criminal.

Another lawyer recently raised controversy for his defense of accused terrorists. David Remes, a partner at Covington and Burling in Washington D.C., represented pro bono a dozen Yemini men held at Quantanamo. At a news conference in Yemen, Remes dropped his trousers to demonstrate the kind of special humiliation experienced by Muslim men forced to undergo routine body searches. A photo of the incident spread quickly over the Web, as readers debated the legitimacy of strip searches for Muslims and the tactical effectiveness of Reme's actions. Although lauding his motives, some leaders of the criminal defense bar were critical of the strategy. According to Monroe Freedman, his action "overwhelmed the fundamental point he was trying to make about the abusive treatment of his clients at Guantanamo. Now the story is him pulling down his pants."[3]

3. Role Morality and Group Identity

Problem 6 raises the question of whether lawyers of color have special responsibilities not to represent clients in practices that injure their racial or ethnic group. The problem, and the questions that follow, are quite straightforward, with the possible exception of Question 4 (page 202), which asks, "Is this a problem of role morality?" The point of the question is that membership in a racial or ethnic group is not a

---

[3] Dan Slater, "Lawyer's Display Lays Bare Debate Over Tactics for Client Advocacy," *Wall Street Journal*, July 23, 2008, at B5.

social role like being a lawyer, which has relatively well-defined responsibilities. Some, but not all, individuals find their race or ethnicity quite central to their sense of identity. It seems open to group members to define the "role" for themselves. On the other hand, it is equally natural to regard an African-American lawyer who represents the Ku Klux Klan to owe a justification over and above what any other lawyer might owe. This response suggests that we do have obligations of loyalty arising from group membership -- in other words, that group membership carries a kind of role morality with it. Many students will respond that if it is wrong for a black lawyer to represent the Ku Klux Klan, or the real estate developer in Problem 6, it must be equally wrong for a white lawyer to do so. Question 2 is meant to suggest to students who have this reaction that it implies a special obligation to support black colleagues, if they protest such representation.

David Wilkins explores these issues in the context of the well-publicized Texas case discussed in the text.[4] Anthony Griffin, an African-American cooperating attorney for the ACLU, agreed to defend, pro bono, Michael Lowe, the grand dragon of the Texas Knights of the Ku Klux Klan. Lowe was protesting, on First Amendment grounds, the state's efforts to compel disclosure of Klan membership lists. Anonymous members of the Klan had been engaged in a campaign to terrorize a small number of blacks in a predominantly white housing project in Vidor, Texas. What attracted particular attention was both Griffin's racial identity and the local NAACP's decision to dismiss him as general counsel for its Port Arthur branch following his acceptance of the case. Griffin argued that his initial decision to represent Lowe was intended primarily to uphold the principle of *NAACP v. Alabama*, 357 U.S. 449 (1959), which ruled that an Alabama court's order requiring the NAACP to turn over its membership lists violated the organization's associational freedom.

Question 3 (p. 205) can be used to supplement the discussion of Problem 6 and the Griffin case. *Stropnicky v. Nathanson* raises the interesting question of whether a female lawyer may decline to accept a male client on ideological grounds. The Massachusetts Commission Against Discrimination thought not, and fined the lawyer for violating anti- discrimination laws. Presumably, if the lawyer argued that her

---

[4] "Race, Ethics, and the First Amendment: Should a Black Lawyer Represent the Ku Klux Klan?" 63 *G. W. L. Rev.* 1030 (1995).

ideology would cloud her independent judgment on behalf of the client, conflict of interest rules (such as Massachusetts' equivalent to Model Rule 1.7(a)(2)) would compel her to decline the representation. It may seem, moreover, that a lawyer with such strong convictions would find it very hard to exercise independent judgment on the male client's behalf. Teachers may ask students whether in this case anti-discrimination law and legal ethics are on a collision course. These materials may be used to raise the question of how much autonomy lawyers ought to have to represent anyone they want, or to decline to do so.

F. Judicial Controls on Adversarial Abuses

Our discussion of adversarial abuse raises several questions about the ethics of advocacy and the adequacy of judicial responses.

Problem 7 raises Rule 11 issues concerning the use of legal procedures merely to delay. It can be discussed in conjunction with Model Rule 3.2, "Expediting Litigation." Often a motion is filed largely to gain time. One paradigm situation arises repeatedly in corporate efforts to defend against hostile takeovers, when lawyers representing the target corporation bring lawsuits to buy time for their client to locate a "white knight." Such delaying tactics are rarely subject to sanctions. However, in sufficiently egregious or unsympathetic cases, courts may impose penalties. In *Davis v. Veslan Enterprises*, 765 F.2d 494 (5th Cir. 1985), for example, the jury in a wrongful death action brought in a Texas state court awarded $13 million to the plaintiff. After plaintiff moved for judgement on the verdict, but before the hearing on that motion, defendant petitioned to remove to federal court. The federal court found that there was no real basis for removal, and that the defendant was simply trying to save money; there could be no entry of judgement until the case was remanded to the state court, and no interest could run until judgment was entered. The federal court imposed sanctions of $5800 in attorney's fees and $33,000 in lost interest. This case may be discussed in class together with the first part of Problem 7. Many students who sympathize with the Legal Aid Defendant will not sympathize with Veslan Enterprises, and vice-versa, even though the issues are quite similar. It is worth exploring whether lawyers' sense of the moral status of their clients' positions should bear on issues of frivolity. *In re Levine*, 847 P.2d 1093 (Ariz. Sup. Ct. 1993), holds that even though a claim may be non-frivolous, pursuing it for an improper motive can subject a lawyer to discipline under Rule 3.1 or 4.4. In that case, the court held that the lawyer's subjective intent in

46

filing lawsuits against his former colleagues should be considered.

The safe-harbor provision of Rule 11, which permits lawyers to withdraw or modify papers within 21 days of a motion for sanctions without penalty, provides an additional opportunity for abuse in Problem 7; it permits the lawyers to buy their client three weeks without risking any penalty -- at which point the lawyers may be able to start over again.

The second part of the problem raises a critical question: Is Rule 11 intended to prevent the use of the courts for personal vindication? Most students rebel against the notion that access to court should be restricted to only those plaintiffs who stand to make money; the establishment of legal principles for their own sake also appears important. This raises questions about litigants who will not be made whole by the remedy they seek because their legal costs outweigh their direct economic benefits. Are these plaintiffs suing simply to harass their adversary? If so, underfunded public interest organizations will be particularly vulnerable to sanctions. Professors may also stress the gatekeeping function of Rule 11 – it helps control caseloads– and draw an analogy to Rule 68, which penalizes plaintiffs who turn down a settlement offer greater than what they ultimately collect at trial. Rule 68 indicates that the justice system is not to be used for legal vindication irrespective of the costs and benefits. However, courts have also recognized a legitimate regulatory and deterrent function of lawsuits in contexts like class actions, where the cost of litigation far exceeds the monetary value to any individual plaintiff.

At the end of the section we raise the related jurisprudential question of what makes a legal argument frivolous. The legal realists often asserted that law is so case- and fact-specific that until a court has ruled on a matter, an argument cannot be said to be legally frivolous.

Students who oppose sanctions generally find this argument attractive, and it is worth bringing up examples of claims that they will have a hard time arguing are non-frivolous. An excellent example is *Vaccaro v. Stephens*, 879 F.2d 866 (9th Cir. 1989). Vaccaro, a slightly-built woman of Spanish and Philippine descent, attempted to use the first-class lavatory while traveling coach class with her husband on a cross-country flight. She was assaulted by Stephens, a large male first-class passenger, who called her a "Chink slut and a whore," told her she was too dirty to use the first-class washroom, and pushed her against a bulkhead. She subsequently sued Stephens, and he counterclaimed, arguing that his first-class ticket conferred on him a license to the first-class lavatory on which she was trespassing, and the donnybrook had injured him by spoiling his flight. His law firm was sanctioned for venturing this argument, and it may be hard to find a student who is willing to disagree.

Another interesting recent case on frivolity is *Storms v. Action Wisconsin, Inc.*, 750 N.W.2d 739 (Wis. 2007), in which a closely divided Wisconsin Supreme Court upheld sanctions against an attorney representing a Christian activist on the grounds that the attorney continued to press a defamation action against a gay rights group when he knew or should have known that the suit had no reasonable basis in fact or law. The case arose out of a speech made by a Louisiana pastor Grant Storms, made in Milwaukee at the "International Conference on Homo-Fascism." Storm's speech called the audience to action, drawing an analogy between the need to combat the gay rights movement and the Biblical account of just war against the Philistines. After the speech, gay rights group Action Wisconsin issued a press release which Storms claimed falsely indicated that he had urged the murder of gays. The press release referred to a portion of Storms's taped sermon in which he said, "Wheeew! Come on. Let's go. God has delivered them all into our hands. Hallelujah! Boom, boom, boom, boom, boom. There's twenty. Whew. Ca-Ching. Yes. Glory. Glory to God. Let's go through the drive-thru at McDonald's and come back and get the rest." Id. at 743-44. Storms sued Action Wisconsin for defamation, claiming that "boom boom boom" was not meant to be the sound of gunfire, while the McDonald's comment really meant that Christian activists should pause in their struggle and take a break. Id. at 750. The trial court sanctioned Storms's attorney James Donohoo on the basis that no non-frivolous argument exists that Action Wisconsin's press release met the legal standard necessary to support a defamation action against a public figure. The dissenting opinion argued that because the law of defamation is unclear and complex, a reasonable attorney might have believed that a jury could find malice.

Problem 8, and the materials on discovery abuse, are worth mentioning in conjunction with the controversial 1994 amendments to Federal Rule 26 providing for "core discovery" (see FRCP, Rule 26(a)(1)). Problem 8 raises an important issue that might be called the "ethics of payback": even if a lawyer does not wish to play hardball, isn't it necessary to do so when the adversary has "started it," in order to avoid exploitation?

In this edition of the textbook, we have replaced the well-known 1993 *Fisons* decision, in which the Washington Supreme Court sanctioned the Seattle firm Bogle & Gates for discovery abuse. We have replaced *Fisons* with the 2008 case *Qualcomm Inc. v. Broadcom Corp.* We have done so for three reasons. First, and perhaps most important, almost no courts outside Washington have ever cited *Fisons* on the issue of sanctioning discovery abuse. In one of the only decisions referring to *Fisons*, the Montana Supreme Court denied the motion for sanctions. *Fjelstad v. State ex rel. Dep't. of Highways*, 883 P.2d 106 (Mont. 1994). Interesting as the *Fisons* case is, it turns out to have made little impact on the law. (Furthermore, many students will have already studied *Fisons* in their 1L civil procedure class.) Second, *Qualcomm* raises issues about electronic discovery that are highly germane to contemporary litigation practice, and which we believe will resonate with law students. Third, *Qualcomm* created a sensation within the organized bar. (One of the authors received an e-mail about the case from the ethics partner at a law firm entitled "Devastating Attorney Misconduct Opinion," which stated: "I've attached a decision by a federal court in California that has gotten a lot of attention this past week. It is an extraordinary opinion in that it sanctions some very well-respected lawyers for discovery abuses in the middle of a contentious trial, and it refers six of them to the California Bar for further discipline. It has become required reading at my firm, and we have sent it to many of our clients as well. It's long and depressing, but well worth reading.")

As the text mentions (page 226), the district judge vacated the sanctions order so that six of Qualcomm's lawyers could dispute it. In the original sanctions hearing, Qualcomm had invoked the attorney-client privilege on many documents, while releasing some that inculpated the attorneys by making it appear that they knew of Qualcomm's deceptions. The attorneys wished to puncture the privilege to permit them to do discovery against Qualcomm to find documents that might show that their client had deceived them. As this book goes to press, the discovery process is still underway, and has become contentious. See *Qualcomm v. Broadcom*, Case No. 05cv1958-B (BLM), 2008 U.S. Dist. Lexis 91104 (Nov. 7, 2008)(granting discovery over Qualcomm's objections, but imposing a protective order on discovered documents because of Qualcomm's continued vulnerability to litigation by Broadcom). Professors who teach this case before teaching the attorney-client privilege should not allow the class to become deflected onto this issue. We would recommend simply saying that Qualcomm's lawyers dispute the facts and that litigation continues over whether Qualcomm deceived them. The important points for discussion – raised in the questions on pages 226-28 – assume that the facts are those in the opinion; professors should make sure that students don't "dodge the hypothetical." Professors should also continue to monitor the ongoing litigation for new developments. Discussion should center on question 1: does *Qualcomm* mean that lawyers will have to do their own electronic searches of client computers? We do not believe so; in our view, the most plausible reading of the case is that lawyers should carefully review the search terms used by clients to make sure that none are omitted; and insist on doing their own search only if client behavior seems evasive. (See the first paragraph on page 226, which emphasizes "numerous warning signs that Qualcomm's document search was inadequate.") Question 3, which asks "Is it proper to infer from a lawyer's resume that he or she is too smart to have been fooled by a client?" can also lead to interesting discussion.

Civility and Civility Codes

Our discussion of civility codes is brief, but we believe that *Lee v. American Eagle Airlines, Inc.* is fun to teach and extremely rich. We have found that the questions following the opinion generate interesting discussion. The judge's sanction against the Kurzban brothers is extraordinary – in effect, fining them more than $300,000 for incivility. So is his rationale, which suggests that incivility reflects a lack of skill that justifies a reduction in standard hourly rates. Students can debate what, if any, sanctions are appropriate for minor incivilities, such as the lawyer who turned to his opponent during a deposition and said, "You are an obnoxious little twit. Keep your mouth shut." The lawyer was in fact fined $200, plus $693 in costs, for this comment.[5]

One line of argument that instructors can use to justify the Kurzbans' over-the-top behavior has been suggested by experienced civil rights litigators: the purpose of the drama may have been to

---

[5] Gerald F. Uelman, *Supreme Folly* 67 (1990).

reassure their client. Often, unsophisticated employees who sue their employers for discrimination are extremely intimidated by their adversaries – so much so that it affects their testimony and allows them to be buffaloed by harsh cross examination. Attorneys who observe that their client is dispirited and frightened may conclude that the only way to give their client courage in the case is to engage in exaggerated chest-bumping behavior like the Kurzbans'.

CHAPTER V: CONFIDENTIALITY AND THE ATTORNEY-CLIENT PRIVILEGE

Doing It Quickly

We believe that the material in this chapter could justify more than a minimum of three classroom hours to treat adequately. But for the minimum three-hour segment, we recommend the following:

First hour: Problem 1, which may include the videotape mentioned below. An overview of Model Rule 1.6, together with the variety of state exceptions to this rule, can accompany what is likely to be a more general discussion about exceptions to confidentiality in extreme cases.

Second hour: Section A on the background of the attorney-client privilege (*excluding* Problem 2); Section C.1 and 2 (on the crime-fraud exception, omitting the Minnesota tobacco case).

Third hour: Section D on the organizational attorney-client privilege, together with section E, on the ethical duty of confidentiality.

Section B, on the justification of the attorney-client privilege, can be done fruitfully in an additional classroom hour; and a fifth hour can be filled by discussing the Minnesota tobacco case (section C.3); the taping of attorney-client communications in terrorism cases (section C.4); or by working through Problem 5.

Chapter VI also considers confidentiality in connection with other issues of candor in the litigation process: client perjury, the concealment of evidence, witness preparation, and the impeachment of opposing witnesses. The rationale for linking the issues, argued forcefully by Monroe Freedman's *Lawyers' Ethics in an Adversary System* (1975), is that perjury, impeachment, and witness preparation problems are intimately connected with the obligation of confidentiality and its underlying policies: lawyers often know that a client's testimony is perjurious, or that an opposing witness is testifying truthfully, or that a client-witness needs to be carefully prepped, on the basis of confidential disclosures by the client.

Because these discussions overlap, some teachers may wish to move certain materials around, for example, by proceeding directly from Problem 1 (the well-known Garrow case) to the confidentiality topics in Chapter VI.

Problem 1

We recommend teaching this problem in conjunction with the readily-available videotape "Ethics on Trial,"[1] which treats the case in some detail. "Ethics on Trial" begins with a five-minute general introduction which should be skipped -- it is unnecessary for the Garrow case, and is quite dated. The Garrow segment itself is about ten minutes long, and includes interviews with attorney Frank Armani, the family members of one of Garrow's victims, the prosecutor in the case, and others. The videotape continues with additional material on confidentiality which should be omitted or shown later. We find it best to reserve one fifty-minute class for the videotape and discussion, which can be based on the questions accompanying Problem 1.

The text accompanying Problem 1 includes a transcript of part of the videotaped interview with Armani, but the power of the video lies not merely in what Armani says but in his personal warmth and his obvious sincerity and anguish over the case. In response to Question 1, we believe that Armani states the issue with considerable clarity. It is a clash between his clear professional obligation and the moral duty to avoid inflicting additional grief on the family of Garrow's victims. The prosecutor, by contrast, offers a confused analysis by distinguishing between merely keeping Garrow's confidences and using them to plea bargain. (We restate his argument in the text, but it appears in the videotape as well.) He objects to plea-bargaining because, in his view, it is contrary to the attorneys' duties as "officers of the court" to try to get a murderer back on the street. His understanding of what it means to be an "officer of the court" runs clearly contrary to EC 7-1 and EC 7-19 of the 1969 Code of Professional Responsibility, both of which insist that "[t]he duty of a lawyer to his client and his duty to the legal system are the same: to represent his client zealously within the bounds of the law" (EC 7-19). But even without referring to these Code sections, professors can point out that the argument begs the question by assuming that no "officer of the court" would try to get a murderer back on the street. No criminal defense lawyer would accept a definition of

---

[1] Available from WETA-TV, Washington, D.C.

"officer of the court" that prevents him or her from seeking acquittals or better deals for their clients even if the clients are indeed murderers.

The book *Privileged Information*, by Tom Alibrandi with Frank Armani (1984), offers additional details about the Garrow case and its personal consequences. For example:

- Armani spent approximately $40,000 on his representation of Garrow and almost destroyed his practice; he received $8,900 in compensation from the state – substantially less than the court stenographer.

- Armani's family paid a price for his principles. His wife and daughters were shunned by friends, harassed by obscene phone-calls, and terrified by a Molotov cocktail left in their back yard.

- Armani's personal life suffered as he became overwhelmed by the pressures and publicity of the case. He responded with alcohol abuse and a work schedule that left no time for other concerns.

Few of those touched by the Garrow case lived happily ever after. Although Armani managed to save his marriage and rebuild his law practice, he also suffered a heart attack and failed to gain a position as a district attorney. Belge was suspended from practice for mishandling an estate, and various prison personnel lost their jobs following Garrow's escape.

Question 3 (p. 239) mentions that during Garrow's trial, Armani learned that Garrow had probably been stalking Armani's daughter at some point in the past. Thus, when Question 2 asks whether Armani should have revealed Garrow's strategy to the police, it is important to realize how terrified Armani may have been about Garrow's escape. In any case, however, it seems clear that Armani would be permitted under the Code of Professional Responsibility prevailing at the time to reveal the information, because doing so was arguably necessary to prevent Garrow from continuing the crime of escape from legal custody. On the other hand, the Model Rules do not permit Armani to reveal the information, unless he had a reasonable basis for believing that Garrow was likely to commit a crime involving death or serious bodily harm. Given Garrow's history, that is a close question.

A. The Background of the Attorney-Client Privilege

Lawyers' duties of silence have three legal sources: ethics codes, agency law, and the law of evidence governing the attorney-client privilege. We omit discussion of the agency law rationale, because it is less important than the others, and because it muddies the waters in an introductory overview. Students naturally tend to confuse the duty of confidentiality and the privilege, and our principal aim in this section is to stress the limited nature of the privilege in order to minimize this confusion.

Problem 2

Under prevailing doctrine, the information about the client's identity is unprivileged. However, revealing the client's identity "directly or by reasonable inference would reveal the content of a confidential communication" (*Restatement*, § 69, cmt.*g*) – the *Restatement*'s version of the so-called "last link" doctrine. Under that doctrine, otherwise-unprivileged information about the client's identity is protected because it would provide the "last link" in a chain of evidence that would smoke out a client confidence. However, the last-link doctrine is disputed and somewhat muddy, and it is by no means a foregone conclusion that a court would follow the *Restatement* on the egregious facts of Problem 2.

The threshold assumption in the problem is that the prosecutor refused the proffered deal; otherwise the client would have pled guilty, and his or her identity would be a matter of public record. A further assumption is either that the prosecutor did not subpoena the client's identity or that the subpoena was quashed by the court. In the actual case, the prosecutor evidently decided not to pursue the matter. It is useful to ask students whether informal assurances by prosecutors that they would not ask for an indictment once the client's identity was known should suffice to pierce any privilege of that identity for purposes of the civil action. As a final question about Problem 2, students may consider the possibility of forbidding the prosecutor who has unsuccessfully attempted to learn the client's identity from initiating prosecution after the identity is revealed in a civil matter.

In the actual case, a Palm Beach, Florida judge upheld the

attorney-client privilege. In his view "If we fail to rule as we do in this case, the result would be the erection of a wall between the public and attorneys."[2] Professor Alan Dershowitz agreed with the ruling: "Think about the reasons for confidentiality: you want people to come to lawyers for help....When a client walks through the door, he assumes he's coming to you in confidence....That means his name, his appearance, his fingerprints. If the judge had ruled the other way, I'd have to say to clients: 'Don't give me your name. Wear a mask. Don't leave fingerprints in my office.'"[3] However, Professor Geoffrey Hazard disagreed. "The confidentiality privilege covers things a client tells an attorney, but does not necessarily cover facts that the attorney finds out or learns from other people....For example, can prosecutors ask questions like how tall is the client? What is the color of his eyes?"[4] Hazard maintained the traditional view that client identity, like physical evidence about clients, is not privileged, because the privilege covers only conversations.

In the Palm Beach case, the police eventually were able to trace the hit-and-run driver, who confessed, and then testified about the accident under a grant of immunity.

---

[2] Quoted in Jeffrey Schmalz, "Lawyer Granted Right to Conceal Client's Identity," Oct. 14, 1988, at A1.

[3] Id.

[4] "Lawyer May Be Forced to Identify Client," *N. Y. Times*, Oct. 13, 1988, at A22.

B. The Justification of the Privilege

Teachers who plan to spend only one or two days on Chapter V, or who wish to emphasize doctrine, may omit this section, which focuses on the conventional rationale for the privilege (as well as the duty of confidentiality). The most common argument for the privilege is instrumental and utilitarian: the privilege is necessary to encourage clients to confide in their attorneys, and full communication is necessary to insure adequate representation and assistance that promotes compliance with the law. On that reasoning, the privilege maximizes the social good. This argument is repeatedly advanced (it appears in EC 4-1 of the 1969 ABA Code, in the Comment to Model Rule 1.6, and in every evidence textbook), but seldom scrutinized. Jeremy Bentham's powerful attack on the privilege, firmly grounded in the very utilitarian arguments that are supposed to justify it, is therefore a very good way to penetrate beneath the usual truisms.

The best place to focus discussion of Bentham's argument is his insistence that there is nothing wrong with chilling disclosures from a guilty defendant to his attorney, even if that leads to an inadequate defense. From Bentham's utilitarian point of view, with its focus on outcomes, the conviction of the guilty is a good result regardless of the process that brings it about. An innocent person, moreover, will have nothing to fear from frank disclosure to his attorney, even without the privilege, so abandoning it assertedly has no down side.

This last assertion is a starting point for challenging Bentham: innocent persons may sometimes withhold exculpatory information because they wrongly believe it will incriminate them. A good example for classroom use is Monroe Freedman's description of a Washington, D.C. woman who shot her husband to death when he attacked her with a knife. Unaware of the law of self-defense, she claimed that a burglar killed her husband; she also withheld the crucial exculpatory fact that her husband had attacked her with a knife because she thought it would suggest that she had killed him.[5] A second well-known (but probably apocryphal) example involves the sentencing hearing of a man convicted of burglary. When the judge asked him if he had anything to say before sentencing, he replied that his conviction was

---

[5] Monroe Freedman, *Lawyers' Ethics in an Adversary System* 4-5 (1975).

really quite unfair, because he had been in jail for a different offense on the day of the burglary. Astounded, the judge asked him why he had not mentioned this fact previously, and he replied: "I was afraid that if I mentioned it you would think I was a criminal."[6]

Bentham's framework might suggest that such cases are too exceptional to justify the privilege, but their facts, together with Bentham's indifference to process concerns, indicate an important flaw in his otherwise-convincing argument. "Better that ten guilty criminals go free than that one innocent person be wrongly convicted" is a principle that is persuasive to many of us, but that is unintelligible to a true utilitarian. The concern for individual rights underpinning that principle is one that Bentham probably would have derided as "nonsense on stilts." The most effective refutation of that approach is likely to rest on arguments based on individual rights and dignity.

A particularly useful update of Bentham's arguments is Daniel Fischel, "Lawyers and Confidentiality," 65 *U. Chi. L. Rev.* 1 (1998). To Bentham's arguments, Fischel adds another utilitarian argument against confidentiality and the privilege: because third parties know that lawyers may well be concealing crucial confidential information, they will be suspicious of lawyers' assertions, which damages the interests of honest, candid clients and benefits only the dishonest.

Rhode's *In the Interest of Justice* 106-115 (2000) provides a critical analysis of the conventional justifications for current confidentiality protections, discussing cases like *Spaulding v. Zimmerman* (life-threatening aneurysm), *Balla v. Gambro* (defective kidney dialysis machine); OPM Leasing (computer leasing fraud); and Leo Frank (innocent man subject to death sentence for client's crime). Her analysis notes that other countries, and this nation for most of its history, made do without the sweeping protections that the bar now claims are essential. In addition to exploring empirical problems with the claim that absolute confidentiality is essential for effective representation, *In the Interests of Justice* surveys ethical problems with the individual rights justification for sweeping confidentiality rules. It is

---

[6] The example comes from Michael D. Bayles, *Professional Ethics* 83-84 (1981).

not self-evident from a moral standpoint why the rights of clients should always trump those of innocent third parties, particularly when the client is an organization.

C. The Crime-Fraud Exception to the Attorney-Client Privilege

Our treatment of the crime-fraud exception to the attorney-client privilege emphasizes three major points: (1) the importance of wrongful client intent; (2) the irrelevance of whether lawyers are aware that the client is consulting them in furtherance of a planned crime or fraud; and (3) the fact that the "past," "ongoing," and "future" crimes need to be defined relative to the time that clients communicate with their lawyer, not the time at which they assert the privilege. A particularly clear statement of this final point appears in *In re Grand Jury Proceedings (FMC Corp.)*, 604 F.2d 798, 803 (3d Cir.1979):

> [T]he district court's finding that "a crime has been committed by [the defendant]"...does not state whether the crime was committed before or after [the defendant's attorney] and his firm were retained for the work during which the documents at issue were generated. If the crime had been completed before retention of the...firm, then the privilege should be in effect. If, however, the crime was a continuing one, or one that occurred after the firm was consulted, then the prima facie showing made by the government would suffice to allow inspection by the grand jury.

The past/ongoing/future-crime (or fraud) distinction is the most common way that lawyers think about when the crime-fraud exception applies. But, as we point out, it is really only a rule of thumb. The real test is whether the attorney-client conversation was "in furtherance of" the client's crime or fraud. In the vast majority of cases, conversations about past crimes aren't in furtherance of them, and professional conversations about future crimes and frauds are, but there will be some cases in which this is not true.

Problem 3 presents a common situation in which most courts are likely to pierce the privilege. True, the defense attorney discussed the income tax situation solely in connection with defending the client for past crimes, and from the defense point of view piercing the privilege appears wholly unjustifiable. However, the client consulted the lawyer in furtherance of an intended income tax evasion, and such

59

criminal activity (like perjury before a grand jury) has for decades been a convenient way to target organized crime figures who are hard to convict for more objectionable offenses. Discussion of the problem may center on how the prosecution could make out a prima facie case that the crime-fraud exception applies. One way would be through independent evidence – for example, testimony by an informant that the defendant had said he had discussed his federal income tax with his defense attorney. Lacking that corroboration, the prosecutor can simply subpoena the defense attorney and ask him or her whether conversations about the client's federal income tax had occurred prior to April 15. Though the defense attorney will assert the privilege, the prosecutor can argue that *if* such conversations occurred, there is good reason to believe that they fall under the crime-fraud exception. If the client discussed his federal income tax with a criminal defense attorney (rather than a tax lawyer), the obvious inference is that he was attempting to learn how his tax reporting would impact his ongoing criminal case, which makes it likely that he was talking about how to handle his illicit income. The teacher should direct students' attention to Model Rule 3.8(e), which attempts to restrict the circumstances under which prosecutors may subpoena defense attorneys. This rule was adopted as a result of complaints by criminal defense lawyers about aggressive use of subpoenas by federal prosecutors. The Department of Justice has traditionally asserted that, under the Supremacy Clause, federal prosecutors are not bound by state court rules such as 3.8(e). This issue is discussed in Chapter VI.

On the other hand, prosecutors with whom we have spoken state that they would not subpoena defense attorneys in situations such as Problem 3 unless the attorney as well as the client is the target of a criminal investigation. This, it should be emphasized, is a matter of prosecutorial discretion or office policy, rather than a point about whether the crime-fraud exception applies as a matter of law.

Teachers might ask whether Armani could have been compelled to answer questions about Garrow's evasion strategies following his escape. Although Garrow's escape was a future crime (from the moment of the conversations), Garrow was surely not talking to Armani with the intention of planning or executing his future escape, so the answer must be "no". Although this is a straightforward question, it may help students understand the practical application of the crime-fraud exception.

Bersani v. Bersani is, as noted, a well-known family law case. It is also quite a confused opinion. At one point, the court seems to be saying that the attorney-client privilege must be pierced because of the best interests of the child – a doctrinal point that seems indefensible. After all, there are often compelling interests in piercing the privilege, and the court makes no attempt to explain why the interests of children alone are sufficient to eliminate the privilege. Elsewhere, the court seems to hold that violating a court order is a fraud – and this is the crucial point of the case. Often, it seems, a court will simply identify "fraud" with "stuff we don't like," which makes the crime-fraud exception very broad indeed. This appears to be the view taken in the *Restatement of the Law Governing Lawyers* § 82, cmt. *d*, quoted on page 257.

Question 2(e), p.257. Compare the two formulas "intentional wrongs involving a client acting with bad faith and intending, or purposely oblivious to, serious harm to another" (Wolfram) and "misconduct fundamentally inconsistent with the basic premises of the adversary system" (*In re Sealed Case*). Which is broader? There is no general answer. Not all misconduct inconsistent with the adversary system intends serious harm to another, so Wolfram's formulation is not broader than the D.C. Circuit's. Conversely, however, not every intentional wrong involving bad faith and intent to harm is inconsistent with the basic premises of the adversary system (although the court never explains what those premises are). Wolfram and the court focus on two different wrongs: harm to other people and harm to the legal system.

However, in cases like *Bersani* where the wrong consists of a lawyer or client violating a court order and concealing the information needed for enforcement of the order, it seems clear that courts could consider the client's conduct "inconsistent with the basic premises of the adversary system" whether or not harm to another person is intended. In such cases, the D.C. Circuit's test is much broader than Wolfram's.

Question 3, p. 257. Under the *Restatement* test, the answer is yes provided that the concealment is knowing or reckless. Under the other tests quoted in Question 2, the answer is no. The Black's Law Dictionary definition is satisfied only if the concealment induces others to act; Wolfram's test requires serious harm to another; and the Model Rules "Terminology" test requires a fraud under state law.

Minnesota Tobacco Litigation

The Minnesota Tobacco Litigation case-study takes students through what was arguably the most momentous use of the crime-fraud exception ever. The important point of the case, emphasized by the parallel drawn with the Dalkon Shield litigation, is that it is an abuse of the attorney-client privilege to create a stricture solely for the purpose of making harmful information disappear into a "black hole" or "cone of silence." Here, attorneys supervised scientists doing sensitive research for two reasons: first, attorneys would know what kind of information is legally damaging, and, second, attorneys could claim that the research reports were privileged. Doctrinally, the reason that this is illegitimate is that the purpose is not to facilitate lawyer-client communication but to shield documents.

Question 1, p. 263. Where is the fraud? The Minnesota court's theory is that a manufacturer has a duty to investigate and disclose product hazards. This seems like an overly broad theory, as the question is meant to indicate. No court has ever held that quietly settling products liability cases and signing secrecy agreements is fraudulent. This question may prompt student responses that what the tobacco companies did was different. It's not just that they tried to keep information about cigarette hazards out of the public's reach; they also argued for years that the hazards of smoking were unproven, knowing that this was untrue. (Or was it? The industry had funded and generated studies casting doubt on the hazards of smoking, so it had created some controversy over the risks.) On this theory, the fraud wasn't the failure to warn the public, but the evasiveness over whether there were genuine hazards to warn the public about.

Question 2, p. 264. How "radical" were the incursions on the privilege? Very! The "sampling" method was unprecedented and purely a concession to practicality. Students can argue about whether such a method satisfy the requirements of justice? Perhaps it can't – but the argument in its favor is that refusing to sample documents, allowing all of them to stay privileged, would be much less just.

Question 3. Teachers can point out that it may be much more dangerous for companies to fail to do appropriate research, since that exposes them to substantial negligence liability.

Question 4 asks why the Minnesota court used two somewhat inconsistent theories to pierce the privilege: the theory that the documents were not privileged in the first place, because they had been communicated to counsel not for litigation purposes but only to shield them from the privilege; and the theory that the crime-fraud exception applies to the documents. One answer to the question is that each theory holds for some documents but not others. Not all documents had been communicated to counsel only to shield them from discovery, and so the second theory was necessary to reach those that had not. Conversely, plaintiffs may not have been able to demonstrate that all documents routinely routed to counsel for purposes of the privilege had been routed in this way in furtherance of fraud.

The saga of the attorney-client privilege and tobacco litigation continued after the events discussed in the text. In June 2004, D.C. District Judge Gladys Kessler, who presided over the Justice Department's RICO case against the tobacco industry,

> ordered the British American Tobacco Co. to turn over a long-sought document that allegedly served as a corporate blueprint for destroying damaging tobacco company records under the guise of document preservation. British American has fought for two years to keep the memo private, raising interest in its contents. U.S. District Judge Gladys Kessler ruled ... that the Australian company could no longer claim the document was protected because the company had engaged in "inexcusable conduct" by initially concealing the memo's existence. The document, known as the "Foyle Memorandum," is considered a potentially important piece of evidence in the federal government's effort to force five tobacco companies to pay $280 billion in damages on charges of racketeering and corruption. The Justice Department is preparing for a September trial in which it accuses the tobacco companies of conspiring to conceal the dangers of smoking from the public and destroying documents that show they knew tobacco could sicken and kill smokers. In her decision, Kessler noted that she was taking the unusual step of imposing a "serious sanction" against British American (BATCo) by waiving the attorney-client privileges the company later claimed in not releasing the memo.[7]

---

[7] Carol D. Leonnig, "Judge Orders Tobacco Firm to Turn Over Key Document," *Wash. Post*, June 2, 2004, A26.

The Foyle Memorandum was drafted by Andrew Foyle, a British lawyer representing BATCo and an Australian subsidiary. Written in 1990, it advised the subsidiary about routing crucial documents to company lawyers to shield them from discovery by claiming privilege. As we noted on page 40 of this teacher's manual, Judge Kessler eventually found the tobacco companies liable of a massive RICO violation. *U.S. v. Philip Morris et al.*, 449 F.Supp.2d 1, 27 (D.D.C. 2006).

To teach the **War on Terror** section, professors should begin by explaining the mechanics of the regulation quoted on pages 265-67. Discussion may then proceed to discuss the policies pro and con. The policy arguments are straightforward. On the side favoring the regulation lies the importance of deterring terrorism. Echoing Bentham's argument from Section B, one might argue that innocent inmates (or innocent conversations) won't be harmed by the regulation, while "guilty" conversations don't deserve to be protected. A simpler version of the argument notes that under the regulation privileged conversations remain privileged, and thus the regulation takes steps to protect the attorney-client privilege. The taping might interfere with the attorney-client *relation*, but it doesn't narrow or eliminate the privilege. Notice that messages that the client transmits to the outside world through the lawyer wouldn't be privileged anyway, because by communicating them to third parties the lawyer would waive the privilege.

But it is important that the prospect of being taped and monitored will interfere with the attorney-client relationship, and that is the chief point on the other side of the argument. The regulation will have a chilling effect on essential lawyer-client communications. Not only are clients likely to be deterred from providing candid answers to questions, but lawyers are likely to be deterred from asking questions where the "wrong" answer might be fatal to the client's case. Furthermore, the fact that the regulation doesn't protect conversations unrelated to legal representation means that attorneys can't even try to build rapport with their clients by asking personal questions, if the answers might be revelations of inner feelings that clients don't want hostile strangers to hear. Granted, such conversations aren't covered by the attorney-client privilege, but without taping that won't matter, because as long as some of the conversation is privileged the entire conversation will be privileged.

Are the safeguards of privileged information adequate? On the one hand, a privilege team reviews tapes to ensure that no privileged information falls into the hands of investigators. Second, the government must provide written notification to the prisoner and his lawyer about the possible monitoring of their conversations. And, finally, monitoring must be ordered by the Attorney General on the basis of information from the head of a federal law enforcement or intelligence agency that reasonable suspicion exists that the prisoner will misuse attorney-client conversations to facilitate terrorism. Without such reasonable suspicion, a report from the head of a federal agency, and the Attorney General's order, no monitoring can take place.

On the other side, teachers should emphasize that the privilege team consists of lawyers on the prosecution rather than the defense side, who are likely to favor the prosecution on close calls, and may in any event make mistakes; furthermore, the regulation permits the privilege team to reveal monitored information if a federal judge approves its revelation (and nothing in the regulation says that the federal judge cannot approve the revelation of privileged information). Finally, if a judge approves secret monitoring, the regulation does not require that either the prisoner or his lawyer be notified; and the question whether a "reasonable suspicion" exists is left to the Attorney General, not to a court.

Question 2 (p. 267), asks whether the regulation states the crime-fraud exception accurately. It holds that a conversation that "facilitates" criminal acts is not privileged. But a conversation may "facilitate" criminal acts without the client intending it to do so (for example, it may give moral support to outside terrorists). The crime-fraud exception traditionally applies only when the client is using the conversation to further a crime or fraud; and so the test given in the regulation is broader than the traditional crime-fraud exception.

In connection with **Question 5 (p. 267)**: The Center for Constitutional Rights launched a Freedom of Information Act lawsuit against the National Security Agency on behalf of lawyers representing Guantanamo inmates who believe they have been illegally wiretapped. The government gave the so-called "Glomar response," asserting that either affirming or denying that NSA wiretapped the attorneys would reveal sensitive national security information. In June 2008, District Judge Denise Cote agreed with the government: *Wilner v. NSA*, 07 Civ. 3883 (DLC), 2008 U.S. Dist. Lexis 48750. Further information about this ongoing litigation is available on CCR's website, http://ccrjustice.org/ourcases/current-cases/wilner-v.-national-security-agency.

D. The Attorney-Client Privilege: Organizational Clients

This section focuses on two related aspects of the corporate attorney-client privilege and duty of confidentiality: (1) the scope of the privilege (the traditional debate between the control group and subject matter tests); and (2) the moral or ethical justifications for maintaining a corporate client's confidences.

The centerpiece of our discussion is *Upjohn v. United States*, which offers an excellent vehicle for exploring the corporate attorney-client privilege. On first exposure, students usually find *Upjohn*'s reasoning close to airtight. Accordingly, the discussion questions attempt to generate critical analysis by probing the Court's underlying logic. Questions 2-4 (pp. 272-73) suggest flaws in each of the Court's three arguments against the control group test. Luban's *Lawyers and Justice: An Ethical Study* 222-28 (1988), provides a more extended critique of the decision which may be useful in class preparation.

Question 1 focuses on the concern expressed in Chief Justice Burger's concurring opinion in *Upjohn*: that the opinion's refusal to lay down a rule gives inadequate guidance to lower courts and corporations. In exploring that issue, a threshold question is how the rationale in *Upjohn* differs from the subject-matter test. Students usually see *Upjohn* as offering a version of the subject-matter test, and thus have trouble answering this question. One plausible response lies in the first part of *Diversified Industries v. Meredith*'s statement of the subject-matter test, quoted just before *Upjohn*: "the communication was made for the purpose of securing legal advice." Justice Rehnquist points out that most lower-level corporate employees will *not* be seeking legal advice during interviews with corporate counsel but rather will be providing information for the attorney to convey to management. *Upjohn* protects such information-giving activities, whereas *Meredith* seems not to. This illustrates the practical difference between the two cases, and also helps students appreciate the force of Justice Rehnquist's argument, which is a clear improvement over *Meredith*. Second, as the question indicates, the subject-matter test restricts the corporate attorney-client privilege to conversations about a subject-matter within the scope of the employee's duties, whereas *Upjohn* does not.

Questions 2 – 6, however, explore certain weaknesses in the

Upjohn framework. Question 6 describes how managers can create a "black hole" by relying on lawyers to investigate corporate practices and then invoking the attorney-client privilege to protect their findings. Students usually find the "black hole" problem the most compelling criticism of the *Upjohn* rule.

In the next section, we cast a skeptical eye on the justifications of the corporate attorney-client privilege. In his treatise on legal ethics, Professor Wolfram observes that "[t]he general theories advanced to support the attorney-client privilege apply only with diminished strength or not at all to a corporate client."[8] As Wolfram notes, however, "despite the absence of a compelling social reason for extending the privilege to corporations and similar bodies, every jurisdiction treats corporations as covered by it."[9] The criticisms that we raise have had little impact on current law apart from the corporate fiduciary exception in *Garner v. Wolfinbarger* and Judge Campbell's maverick opinion in *Radiant Burners.* A useful focus for discussion is whether efforts to restrict the privilege in corporate contexts are socially desirable or politically possible.

Issues surrounding waiver of the organizational privilege have become increasingly contested. After this chapter went to press, Deputy Attorney General Mark Filip issued a new policy prohibiting federal prosecutors from asking companies under investigation to disclose information normally covered by the privilege and work product protections. The Policy also prevents prosecutors from considering in their charging decisions whether a company has entered into a joint defense agreement with employees subject to investigation or has agreed to pay their fees. However that policy has not halted further efforts to protect the privilege by a coalition including the ABA, the Association of Corporate Counsel, 19 state and local bar organizations, and many former Justice Department officials and U.S. attorneys. That coalition seeks passage of the Attorney-Client Privilege Protection Act, which provides safeguards that could not be revoked by the Justice Department and that would also apply to to other federal agencies including the SEC and EPA.[10]

---

[8] Charles Wolfram, *Modern Legal Ethics* 283 (1986).

[9] Id. at 284

[10]Mark Hanswen, "Memo to Prosecutors: Time to Back Off," *ABA J.,*

On the issue of whether corporate directors should be able to compel the corporation to waive the privilege, Kressel argues in the Note cited on p. 277, n. 91, that it is unfair to allow a defense based on advice of counsel that cannot be properly tested. The articles by O'Sullivan and Richman cited in note 88, pages 276-77, are useful for professors seeking further background and discussion on this issue.

E. The Ethical Duty of Confidentiality

We begin this section by stressing once again the much broader protection of client confidences granted by the Code and Model Rules than by the attorney-client privilege. In particular, we focus on the very narrow range of circumstances in which the Model Rules permit an attorney to reveal confidences in order to protect the interests of third parties from wrongful client actions. After summarizing the controversy over the disclosure requirements in the Model Rules, we turn to the egregious facts in *Spaulding v. Zimmerman* -- a powerful teaching tool despite the fact that it has become something of a casebook chestnut.

Questions 3(b) and (c) in the notes following *Spaulding* are of particular value. We have found that students generally blame either Spaulding's lawyer (for not having learned of the medical reports through discovery), or Dr. Hewitt Hannah (who reported on Spaulding's aneurism to Zimmerman's counsel but not to Spaulding). Such deflections of responsibility enable most students to insist that Zimmerman's counsel was not to blame. Many students are quite conflicted about the case and many are simply avoiding the unpleasant issue by retreating to the "adversary system excuse": "it's not up to Spaulding's adversary to safeguard his interests, it's up to Spaulding's lawyer. That's what the adversary system is all about."

It is often productive to explore with students whether their own moral and reputational concerns should affect their discussion with the client about whether to disclose the condition and their determination about whether to withdraw from representation or leak the adverse information if the client refuses. Students can be pressed to consider

---

November 2008, at 26.

how they would feel if the plaintiff dies of the undisclosed conditions or if it becomes public that they knew of the condition and did not disclose it.

Spaulding pushes most students to agree that there comes a point when confidentiality must give way to conscience; at that point, to paraphrase Shaw, a teacher may point out that all that remains is to dicker over the price -- that is, over the point where conscience kicks in.

F. Confidentiality and Client Fraud

The materials on client fraud center around a problem based on the well-known OPM case, followed by a brief history of the most notorious episodes of lawyers caught up in client frauds over several decades: the *National Student Marketing* case, the savings and loan debacle and the Kaye, Scholer case, and, more recently the accounting scandals such as Enron. Because the lawsuits involving Enron's outside counsel were settled, many facts concerning their role remain confidential, so we have not focused on that case in the discussion. Most of our questions concern another prominent example involving Kaye, Scholer. We have found Professor William Simon's article "The Kaye Scholer Affair: The Lawyer's Duty of Candor and the Bar's Temptations of Evasion and Apology," 23 *Law and Social Inquiry* 243 (1998), particularly useful in preparing to teach this material.

OTS insisted that since Kaye, Scholer had interposed itself between the bank examiners and Lincoln Savings, the firm assumed all the duties of candor incumbent on the regulated institution itself. Professor Hazard's expert opinion rejects that position. It bears note that the opinion was actually written by Kaye, Scholer, together with a stipulation of the facts on which it was based, then reviewed and signed by Professor Hazard. It argued that Kaye, Scholer was acting as traditional litigation counsel, and thus that the firm could properly advocate the client's position, without undertaking an independent investigation.

Problem 4 is based on the well-known OPM case. Though the problem presents the essential facts of the case, we recommend the two articles cited in the accompanying footnote which fill in the background and include numerous poignant details.

A threshold issue is whether OPM's frauds were past? If so,

could Singer Hutner disclose them? It is essential to remind students of the timing element in the crime-fraud exception to the attorney-client privilege. Under the privilege, OPM's frauds were *not* past, because the firm's assistance occurred before and during their commission. Moreover, the firm's ignorance is irrelevant for the crime-fraud exception: only client intent is relevant. Thus, the attorney-client privilege clearly did *not* protect Singer Hutner's knowledge about OPM's frauds.

Singer Hutner's consultants obviously thought that a wholly different analysis was appropriate for the ethical duty of confidentiality. The rules governing Singer Hutner's conduct were the New York Code of Professional Responsibility, which closely tracked the ABA's Code. DR 4-l0l(C)(3) states that "[a] lawyer may reveal the intention of his client to commit a crime and the information necessary to prevent the crime." The most natural reading of this rule suggests that its purpose is solely crime-prevention, and that after the crime has been committed, the lawyer may no longer reveal "the intention of his client to commit a crime." However, the rule does not actually *say* this, and one way of analyzing the situation would be to interpret the exception along the lines of the crime-fraud exception to the attorney-client privilege. On that reading, DR 4-l0l(C)(3) declares that the intention of a client to commit a crime is simply not protected by lawyer-client confidentiality even after the crime is committed, just as the attorney-client privilege does not protect such an intention.

This is clearly a rather strained reading of DR 4-l0l(C)(3). A more promising avenue lies in DR 7-102(B)(l): "A lawyer who receives information clearly establishing that his client has, in the course of his representation, perpetrated a fraud upon a person...shall promptly call upon his client to rectify the same, and if his client refuses...he shall reveal the fraud to the affected person...except when the information *is protected as a privileged communication*" (emphasis added). ABA Formal Opinion 341 interprets "privileged communications" to refer to confidences and secrets as defined in DR 4-101(A), and under this interpretation Singer Hutner cannot reveal the past frauds. However, a court might well disagree with the ABA's reading of "privileged communication" and take it to refer only to communications protected under the attorney-client privilege -- in which case the crime-fraud exception applies.

At this point, it is helpful to direct students' attention from the

Code to the Model Rules. Older versions of Model Rule 1.6 clearly would have forbidden OPM's counsel from revealing either past or future frauds. However, under the current version, MR 1.6(b)(1) and (2) would have permitted Singer Hutner to reveal OPM's future *and past* frauds in which Singer Hutner's services had been used.[11]

The Model Rules also clearly permit withdrawal under Singer Hutner's circumstances, because the clients' conduct gives the lawyers reason to believe that they are continuing in fraudulent conduct. MR 1.16(b)(2). Once they become certain that this is so, MR 1.16(a)(1) in fact *requires* the lawyers to withdraw.

OPM also raises broader issues of organizational culture. The overwhelming evidence is that Singer Hutner never "knew" that the loans it was closing for OPM were fraudulent, even after the first set of revelations, because the firm was trying hard not to know. OPM was its most important client, and Singer Hutner had apparently elected to see no evil. If the firm policy was to learn that it had closed fraudulent loans only after the fact, so that the information was protected under the Code, its excuse seems quite feeble, and this bears emphasis in class. Indeed, applying the criminal law doctrine of wilful ignorance would suggest that Singer Hutner was indeed culpable, and students are likely to disagree about whether that doctrine should apply to lawyers. Notice, however, that the wilful ignorance doctrine has no counterpart in the Model Rules: under the MR, "knowledge" means actual knowledge. See MR 1.0(f).

Professors who want to take up government lawyers' whistleblowing obligations could consult Kathleen Clark, "Government Lawyers and Confidentiality Norms," 85 Wash. U. L. Rev. 1033 (2007). This article concerns Jesselyn Radack, a lawyer in the Justice Department's Office of Professional Responsibility. Radack reviewed interrogation plans for John Walker Lindh, the "American Taliban" who was captured in Afghanistan. When she learned that despite her warnings government

---

[11] On the older version, see Ted Schneyer, "Professionalism as Bar Politics: The Making of the Model Rules of Professional Conduct," 14 *Law & Soc. Inq.* 677, 723-24 (1989).

authorities denied Lindh's *Miranda* rights – and, in fact, tortured him – she attempted to rectify the wrongdoing through channels, and when that failed blew the whistle to reporters. Radack's 2004 book, *Canary In the Coal Mine*, is extremely interesting.

G. Putting It All Together: A Final Problem

The aim of this problem is to give students a realistically difficult analytical exercise, **Problem 5**. If you choose to use the problem in class, it is worth taking at least half an hour to explore its complications.

CANRA, including its exemption for attorneys, is typical of child abuse reporting statutes in many states. So too is the interaction between CANRA, the law governing attorney-client privilege, and the rules of professional conduct. To answer the various questions, we address two preliminary issues:

1. Is your information about your client privileged? First, consider the question without taking into account the crime-fraud exception. Your conversations with the client's daughter are unprivileged, because they are not attorney-client communications. However, your conversations with your client all involve legal advice-giving, and thus are prima facie privileged.

The first conversation with your client, in which you warned her that leaving the children home alone may constitute neglect, is not in furtherance of the crime of neglect. However, the third conversation, in which she called you to ask how much of the burn incident she must reveal, seems (in light of her persistence in leaving the children alone even after your warning) like a step in furtherance of neglect, and possibly in furtherance of a contemplated fraud against her husband and the court. Although the issue is debatable, this conversation seems to fall under the crime-fraud exception, and thus is not privileged. The second conversation, in which she admits that she left the children while she went to care for Shane, falls between the two, can be argued either way.

2. Is your information about your client confidential? After the third conversation, the attorney may reasonably believe that the client will continue to neglect her children. (Fool me once, shame on you; fool me twice, shame on me.) If so, revealing the pattern of neglect is arguably the only way to prevent the crime, and the exception to Rule 1.6 implies that the information is not protected. (It is important to emphasize to students that the hypothetical jurisdiction's version of 1.6 contains a broader exception than the corresponding Model Rule. This is a useful way to emphasize to students that in practice they will need to learn their own jurisdiction's rules, not the Model Rules.) Buttressing this conclusion is the fact that the neglect has led to injury for one child – this is not a case in which the future crime you aim to prevent is inconsequential.

Does CANRA require you to report the child neglect to the authorities? The two conversations with your client's daughter, and at least one (possibly two) conversations with your client, are unprivileged, and thus the reporting exemption for information protected by the attorney-client privilege does not apply. If that were the only basis for exemption, you would be obligated to report the evidence of neglect.

Thus, the issue turns on the other grounds for exemption in CANRA, namely that fulfilling the reporting requirement "would be disclosing matter communicated in confidence by a client to the client's attorney or other information relating to the representation of the client." Here there is room for argument both ways. Undoubtedly, everything your client told you was "communicated in confidence"; but, as we have seen, it is not protected by the confidentiality rule, because it falls under one of the exceptions to the rule. So too, the conversations with the child, which are "information relating to the representation of the client" are not protected by Rule 1.6. Thus, if the exemption-clause of CANRA is interpreted through reference to Rule 1.6 – in our view, the most plausible interpretive strategy – none of this information is exempt, and CANRA requires disclosure. If, on the other hand, the terms "communicated in confidence" and "other information relating to the representation of the client" in the exemption-clause are interpreted independently of Rule 1.6, it continues to apply. In that case, CANRA will not require disclosure; however, Rule 1.6 clearly *permits* disclosure, and one issue to discuss with students is whether the situation is serious enough that a lawyer should use that permission.

An important practical fact is that child abuse reporting statutes are often drafted carelessly, requiring persons to report the crime of child abuse or neglect, but exempting privileged information, despite the fact that often information about child abuse falls under the crime-fraud exception and thus fails to be privileged. In such cases, it seems likely that the drafters simply did not think about the crime-fraud exception. If the crime-fraud exception usually devours the attorney exemption to child abuse reporting, why is the exemption there? This point is worth raising with students.

What about future settlement negotiations? Here, the controversial proposition to discuss with students is that both the burn incident and other evidence of neglect must be disclosed to the wife and her attorney. Model Rule 4.1(b) provides that "a lawyer shall not knowingly fail to disclose a material fact to a third person when disclosure is necessary to avoid assisting a criminal or fraudulent act by a client, unless disclosure is prohibited by Rule 1.6." If you pursue the client's custody claim, the questions are (a) whether doing so without disclosure assists the crime of child neglect; and (b) whether doing so without disclosure assists a fraudulent settlement. As to (a), the problem stipulates that the client does not really desire custody, but (the professor may argue) so long as the lawyer presses the custody claim in negotiations, the possibility of custody is still in play. As to (b), the client is attempting to obtain a better financial deal from his wife by making a credible threat of a custody battle. Under the common law of both contract and tort, negotiating an agreement without disclosure of material facts constitutes fraud; this issue is treated in Chapter VIII.

Finally, what about future dealings with the court? Here there are two questions. First, can the lawyer make any representations to the court about the fitness of the client to have custody of the children without disclosing the evidence of neglect? (Here the answer seems clearly no.) Second, can the lawyer present a settlement agreement in which the custody issue has been a bargaining-chip to the court without violating Rule 3.3(a)(2)? Here, the answer seems to be no, for the same reason that the lawyer should not negotiate the settlement without disclosure, given Rule 4.1(b).

Many students are likely to be troubled by the fact that the attorney has made a claim for child custody knowing that the client's demand for custody is in bad faith. Isn't that in and of itself a fraud? We agree with such students that custody blackmail is ethically troubling, and refer to the materials in Chapter VIII. But, as a legal matter, a bad faith custody demand is not fraudulent. A mother has a legal right to request custody, and the lawyer can often argue that the evidence supports a conclusion that maternal custody represents the best interests of the children in this case.

CHAPTER VI: THE CRIMINAL PARADIGM

This chapter begins with problems central to legal ethics in criminal defense: defending guilty clients, impeaching truthful testimony, suborning perjury, concealing evidence, and coaching witnesses. Some of these problems, of course, face advocates in civil as well as criminal cases, and our title "the criminal paradigm" is meant to reflect a background assumption of the chapter: that zealous advocacy even in non-criminal contexts is modeled on ideals drawn from the criminal defense function. The chapter concludes with ethical problems in criminal prosecution. These, too, are paradigmatic, in the sense that the prosecutor's injunction to seek justice, not victory, exemplifies alternatives to neutral partisanship just as the criminal defense mandate of zealous advocacy exemplifies neutral partisanship in its purest form.

The criminal defense problems should be treated in a minimum of two classroom hours, and could be expanded to four: one on defending the guilty (section A), one on client perjury (section B.1) and concealing physical evidence (section C.1), one on impeaching truthful testimony (section B.2), and one on concealing documentary evidence (section C.2) and coaching witnesses (section C.3). Those teachers who have elected to omit material in Chapter IV on neutral partisanship may wish to devote more attention to section A, which provides independent arguments about the neutral partisanship ideal in criminal defense.

Section A summarizes the justifications for zealous advocacy. Most emphasize the importance either of monitoring the process to protect the innocent, or of insuring that even the guilty are accorded dignity, respect, and procedural regularity. A contrary view, one shared by the general public, is set forth in Marilyn vos Savant's column, "Ask Marilyn," and in the quote from Richard Posner in the Notes (pages 312-13). We have also included a gritty column by *Washington Post* feature writer Henry Allen, which supplements the material on the problems of low-end criminal defense with a much more sympathetic portrait of Washington, D.C.'s court-appointed lawyers. A well-known article by Randy Bellows also describes in moving detail the emotional toll on public defenders. As he puts it, "I am sick of being afraid to walk in my own parking lot yet helping people who mug citizens in other parking lots. I have lost much of the empathy I once had for my clients. It is time to go." [1]

Issues concerning the destruction and fabrication of evidence have become increasingly relevant over the last decade, as growing numbers of in-house counsel and respected law firms have been sanctioned for such abuses. In some instances, the explanation for misconduct is obvious: consider, for example, the statement concerning concealment and misrepresentation in the Dalkon Shield case ("your conscience doesn't pay your salary.")[2] But as the excerpt from *Defending White-Collar Crime* indicates, some attorneys' strategies for avoiding moral responsibility appear to be rooted in principled appeals to the nature of the adversary system.

The defense lawyers that Mann studied were an elite group, consisting mainly of former federal prosecutors with an insider's knowledge of how to frustrate prosecutorial objectives. Other "information control" techniques they enumerated include:

- "helping a person . . . draw facts out of his or her recollection through a creative process (Mann, at 58);

- preventing a client from going before a grand jury because "otherwise he won't come out alive" (Mann, at 135);

- having the client transfer all financial records to an affiliated accountant who will meet with government investigators on the client's behalf and, "like a periscope, scout out the government's case," without revealing his affiliation" (Mann, at 133);

---

[1] Randy Bellows, "Notes of a Public Defender," in Philip B. Heymann and Lance Liebman, *The Social Responsibilities of Lawyers: Case Studies,* 79, 97 (1988).

[2] S. Perry & J. Dawson, *Nightmare: Women and the Dalkon Shield* 205 (1985).

- invoking the attorney-client privilege even when "current legal doctrine . . . tended not to support [its] . . . applicability." (Mann, at 141).

These readings can provide an occasion not only for exploring the conventional justifications for lawyers' neutral partisanship, but also for raising broader questions about the system that encourages such norms. For a thoughtful argument that the existing criminal justice process provides too many advantages for defendants who can afford to exploit them and too little protection for the masses of cases resolved through plea bargains or summary processes, see William Simon, "The Ethics of Criminal Defense," 91 *Mich. L. Rev.* 1703 (1993), as well as a now-dated but still classic article by John Griffiths, "Ideology in Criminal Procedure or a Third 'Model' of the Criminal Process," 79 *Yale Law. J.* 359 (1970). For a more recent overview that takes account of Simon's concerns, but also considers the special justifications for partisanship in criminal cases, see Rhode, *In the Interests of Justice*, at 68-77. For an overview of underfunding, caseload pressures, inadequate oversight, and political biases in indigent defense systems, see Chapter VI in Rhode's *Access to Justice* 122-44 (2004). The chapter includes detailed discussion of current problems and proposed responses that can enliven class discussion: e.g.

- a recent Georgia legislative decision to spend twice as much on improvements for one highway interchange as on the state's entire criminal defense budgets;

- contract lawyers who plead 300 cases without even taking one to trial;

- many judges' disinclination to appoint attorneys who clutter their dockets with motions and trials so that the surest way not to get indigent defense work is to do it effectively.

In fall 2008, as this manual went to press, pubic defenders in at least seven states were refusing to take new cases or were suing to limit caseloads. An increase in prosecutions, a decrease in budgets, and an escalation in penalties that created disincentives for pleas, all contributed to a crisis in indigent defense. In Miami Dade County, the average annual felony caseload had increased to about 500 and misdemeanors to 2225, causing a Florida judge to permit the office to refuse to represent defendants on lesser felony charges. Still, on a typical morning, a Miami prosecutor who had 155 current clients juggled arraignments and plea bargains for 23 defendants, most of whom he had not met before.[3]

For professors who wish to explore the complexities of using "ineffective assistance of counsel" claims as a method for policing defense counsels' performance, the *Rompilla* case noted on p. 321 is worth exploring. It is not entirely clear that examining the file of earlier convictions would have revealed signs of mental health difficulties and alcoholism, and childhood abuse. Nor is it without significance that the information failed to surface from interviews with the defendant, his family members, or three mental health experts. As the dissent noted, case files can be voluminous– trial transcripts, forensic evidence, exhibits, presentence reports etc. and the attorney's office had only two investigators for 2000 cases.

---

[3] Erik Eckholm, "Citing Workload, Public Lawyers Reject New Cases," *N.Y. Times*, November 9, 2008, at A1.

B. Truthful Witnesses and Lying Clients

1. Perjury

We find that Monroe Freedman's "perjury trilemma" still provides the best analytical framework for discussing the client perjury problem. Many teachers erroneously assume that *Nix v. Whiteside*, together with Model Rule 3.3(a)(4) and ABA Formal Opinion 353, have settled the client perjury question. This overlooks the fact that many jurisdictions, including California, Washington, D.C., and New York, still forbid lawyers from revealing client perjury. And there is considerable division of views among courts as to how much evidence lawyers must have, and how convinced they need to be, before concluding that a client's testimony is (or will be) perjurious.

Those jurisdictions that do not require lawyers to reveal client perjury typically do require the lawyer to attempt to persuade the client to reveal the perjury. To illustrate graphically how awkward this can be, we have found it useful to role-play. The instructor takes the role of the perjurious client, and asks a student to take the role of the lawyer telling the client that he must reveal his perjury to the judge. The instructor should stipulate that revealing the perjury will turn a promising case into a sure-thing loss, or even a trip to jail. (The simple fact-pattern in Problem 1(e), page 324, would be an example.) Then, playing the role of client, the instructor should act incredulous and uncooperative when the student tells him or her to reveal the perjury.

The facts of several lower court cases could make for engaging hypotheticals in class discussion. One is *State v. McDowell* (Wis. 2003), discussed in 19 *ABA/BNA Lawyers Man. Prof. Conduct* 443 (2003). There, a a defendant charged with violent sexual assault claimed that the reason his semen was found at the site of the rape was that he had voluntary sexual relations with his girlfriend at this location earlier in the evening. Inconsistencies between McDowell's version and that of his girlfriend caused the attorney to doubt that account and to decide not to have her testify. Those doubts were increased when McDowell reportedly told the attorney that "I'll say what I need [to] say to help myself out and if I have something untruthful I'll say that. I need to help myself out." During the trial, the attorney raised his perjury concerns with the judge, who declined to allow him to withdraw but agreed that if the defendant insisted on testifying, the attorney could permit him to do so in narrative form. After conferring with the client, the attorney told the judge that he had no reason to believe that his client would testify untruthfully. When the trial resumed, the attorney told McDowell to tell his story in narrative form. The Wisconsin Supreme Court held that such an action constituted ineffective representation because the attorney had opted for the narrative approach before perjury required him to do so and because he had not advised his client of that plan. However, the Court also found that the deficient performance was harmless in light of the overwhelming evidence of guilt and the defendant's "preposterous" explanation for the presence of his semen at the crime scene.

A similar holding is *United States v. Midgett*, 342 F.3d 321 (4th Cir. 2003). There, the defendant was convicted of crimes involving a robbery in which the victim was also splashed with gasoline and set on fire. The defendant maintained that he had been in a drug- induced sleep in the back of the vehicle when the crime was committed by a friend of the codefendant. The defendant's attorney found no evidence to corroborate this account, and the codefendant who testified denied that any third party was involved. The trial judge refused to let the attorney withdraw and gave the defendant the choice of representing himself or agreeing to his counsel's refusal to let him testify. He reluctantly chose the later course and the Fourth Circuit reversed his conviction. In the appellate panel's view, "Far fetched as [the client's] story might have sounded to the jury, it was not his lawyer's place to decide that [the client] was lying and to declare his opinion to the Court." For a similar ruling, see *People v. Darrett*, (N.Y. Sup. Ct. App. Div. 2003), 20 *ABA/BNA Lawyers Manuel on Professional Conduct* 12 (2004). Professors can use these cases as hypotheticals to ask students what they would do as lawyers or judges.

The lawyer quoted on p. 331 who predicted that "everyone lies" in criminal cases was arrested for contempt of court. It is not clear whether the prediction held true at his own proceeding.

The remaining sections, on impeachment of the truthful victim, possession of evidence, document retention and destruction, and witness preparation, are quite straightforward to teach, and professors may wish to select only a subset of them or move through all of them quickly. We particularly recommend using the excerpt from Kenneth Mann's *Defending White-Collar Crime*, which presents the very typical defense strategy of "don't ask, don't tell": avoidance of information that would prevent defense lawyers from arguing advantageous theories in discussions with prosecutors. Defense lawyers frequently stress the importance of framing questions to defendants very narrowly, in order to protect their ignorance and preserve their deniability.

The material on impeaching rape complainants also works very well. It bears note that the strategy is not limited to rape cases. A still widely discussed case in point involved the 1988 New York "preppie murder" prosecution. There Jack Litman attempted to defend his ivy league client on charges of murdering his girlfriend, Jennifer Levin, by introducing passages from her diary indicating a taste for "kinky" and aggressive sex. Litman's claim was that his client killed Levin in self-defense during "rough sex." The *American Lawyer* credited Litman as being the "hands down winner" of the "Now You Know Why People Hate Lawyers" award. David Margolick, "At the Bar," *N.Y. Times*, Jan. 22, 1988, at 4.

Problem 3

Answers to the questions raised in this Problem appear in the accompanying note material. The chief point of emphasis is that the attorney's obligations depend on statutes other than the ethics rules, and that these vary by jurisdiction. In some states, it is unlawful to destroy evidence if a proceeding is pending; in others, it is unlawful to destroy the evidence whether or not a proceeding is pending. The most plausible answers are as follows:

a. The lawyer must turn the evidence over (*Ryder*). However, the lawyer should not reveal the source of the evidence (*Meredith*).

b. The lawyer must turn the evidence over.

c. Logically, the answer should be the same as (a); but, as the Notes explain, the *Olwell* rule is seldom invoked with respect to documents in a white-collar case.

d. Because of the duty of confidentiality, the attorney must take no action.

Question 2, p. 343

Arguably, the cases are consistent with Garrow, where the attorneys did not alter or remove the evidence.[4] The obvious distinction between receiving evidence and photographing it is that photographing the evidence does not remove it or prevent its subsequent discovery.

Problem 4

Should Goulden's loose-lipped "superlawyer" keep his law license? One defensible answer is "no" – because he has outrageously violated confidentiality by pointing out his client to Goulden and then revealing an embarrassing confidential conversation. What about his conversation with the client? Certainly if he had expressly told the client to destroy incriminating documents he would have violated Model Rule 8.4(d) by engaging in conduct that is prejudicial to the administration of justice. The conduct may also be criminal, which would, in turn, violate 8.4(b). Students can consider whether his less explicit suggestion is qualitatively different from a direct instruction, and how it compares with Nancy Temple's memo. Whether Temple could be subject to disciplinary proceedings is also worth discussing. Jurors in the Andersen obstruction case stated afterward that their basis for convicting Andersen was not Temple's e-mail about document destruction, but rather other evidence—an e-mail she wrote suggesting self-serving changes in a press

---

[4] Actually, they moved scattered parts of one murder victim's body slightly so that it could be photographed. In teaching this question, it is probably simplest to stipulate that they merely photographed the bodies without touching them.

release. Most commentators believed that the edits in the press release were legitimate

Problem 5 (pp. 351-52) concerns the limits of witness preparation. The fact pattern concerns a witness who gives weak answers, including answers on scientific issues. (To make it concrete, the instructor might stipulate that the witness is a physician discussing details of medical treatment.) The subparts of the question reveal how permissive the standards under MR 3.3(a)(3) are. As long as the witness's answers are truthful, the rule does not forbid the lawyer from eliciting them, nor from preparing the witness to offer them. Thus, telling him to avoid technical terminology, or rehearsing him to be sure that if he uses it he gets it right, does not violate the rule (part (a)). In part (b), the Model Rule does not forbid counseling the client to leave out certain testimony, as long as the testimony he offers is true. Even if the remaining testimony is a misleading half-truth, it does not violate the ethics rule so long as it is not outright false; nor does it constitute perjury – see *U.S. v. Bronston*, 409 U.S. 352 (1973), which determined that in an adversarial setting, it is the adversary counsel's responsibility to elicit the whole truth through follow-up questions. The Court reversed a perjury conviction for a man who offered misleading half-truths.

The second question – whether the lawyer can explain the legal theory of the case to the witness so that he better understands why certain ways of phrasing his testimony will be damaging – sounds very much like the familiar *Anatomy of a Murder* problem. But there is one crucial difference: in the latter, the lawyer explains the law to a witness who is then better able to offer false testimony. Here, so long as the client testifies truthfully (albeit in different words than those he would have chosen on his own), the lawyer is neither enabling a fraud on the court nor offering false evidence.

The third question in part (b) is slightly more difficult. If the lawyer proposes alternative phrasing, he or she must be careful that the witness agrees (without pressure from the lawyer) that it represents the witness's beliefs. Otherwise, the lawyer has suborned perjury: the federal perjury statute, for example, finds the crime where a witness under oath "states or subscribes any material matter which he does not believe to be true" (18 U.S.C. § 1621(1)). Thus, a lawyer who persuades a witness to testify in words that the witness believes to be untrue (even if the lawyer believes that the proposed phrasing is equivalent to the witness's) has induced the witness to violate the perjury prohibition. (We are supposing here that the witness protests to the lawyer that he doesn't agree with the proposed phrasing.) Even though this does not, strictly speaking, violate MR 3.3(a)(3) – because the lawyer does not know that the testimony is false, and indeed may believe that it is true – suborning perjury is a crime, and therefore prohibited by MR 1.2(d), 8.4(b), and 8.4(d). The same considerations apply in answering part (d) of the problem. While the lawyer may suggest to the client which topics questions are meant to elicit – e.g., "When I ask you 'what happened next?' be sure you mention the phone call to your mother that you told me about" – putting words in the client's mouth runs a strong risk of suborning perjury.

No rule prohibits the lawyer from insisting that the witness testify through an interpreter if the lawyer thinks the fact-finder will be distracted or annoyed by the witness's accent or voice.

What makes this problem illuminating is that all of proposed forms of witness preparation will arguably confer a false credibility to the client's testimony, a fact that may deeply trouble students.

For further discussion of the adversarial ethics encouraging document destruction, see the materials on discovery abuse in Chapter IV and ethics in organizational settings in Chapter VII.

D. Prosecutorial Ethics

The second half of this chapter raises ethical issues in criminal procedure from the other side. Like court-appointed defense lawyers, prosecutors enjoy substantial decision-making autonomy and confront substantial caseload pressures and funding constraints. However, prosecutors also seek to "do justice" for constituencies whose interests are not always coextensive. In prosecutorial contexts, conflicts often arise between procedural and substantive fairness as well as among more specific objectives such as protecting the public, responding to victims, safeguarding constitutional rights, deterring offenses, and encouraging rehabilitation. All of these may be counterbalanced by prosecutors' own interests, such as maintaining a high conviction record, managing their caseloads, gaining favorable publicity, and so forth.

An interesting debate on prosecutors' obligations to do justice appears in an exchange from the 1996 *Georgetown Journal of Legal Ethics*, cited on p. 357, n. 109. In the first article, Kenneth Bresler, a former Assistant District Attorney and then federal prosecutor, criticizes the tendency of prosecutors to measure success in terms of win-loss records. In the response, Thomas Hagerman, a former Assistant U.S. Attorney, dismisses such views as "naive." In his experience, "Prosecutors who work hard do so because:

> 1) they want to do the right thing;
>
> 2) having done the right thing and charged the right people, they want to convict them, in short, to win; and
>
> 3) having won, they want to be recognized – by peers, publicity, awards, supervisors, slots, subsequent judicial appointments, and, in their finest hours, book tours."[5]

Students can consider whether these motives are always as consistent and benign as Hagerman suggests, and if not, what to do about it.

Prosecutorial ethics is a less familiar subject to most professional responsibility teachers than criminal defense. Professors wishing to treat the subject in just one or two classroom hours should probably focus on **Problems 6, 9**, and **11**, assigning with them the following readings: The ABA Standards on the Prosecution Function, Uviller's article, the notes on plea bargaining and the notes on disclosure obligations.

Problem 6

---

[5] "I Never Lost a Trial: When Prosecutors Keep Score of Criminal Convictions," 9 *Geo. J. Legal Ethics* 537 (1997); "Confessions From a Scorekeeper: A Reply to Mr. Bresler," 10 *Geo. J. Legal Ethics* (1996).

Problem 6 and the related questions are loosely based on federal prosecutor Jay Stephens's campaign against Washington, D.C. Mayor Marion Barry, who was convicted in 1990 for drug offenses after a sting operation. His conviction was the culmination of a lengthy investigation initially motivated not by Barry's drug use but by suspicions about corruption in his administration. In discussing standards of proof, it is worth emphasizing that prosecutors generally have practical, if not ethical reasons for bringing a case only if they are convinced of the defendant's guilt. As former Assistant U.S. Attorney John Kaplan once noted, most of his colleagues believed that "there are enough cases we can win without bringing any of the other kind."[6]

Yet while such considerations may deter a prosecutor from trying a dubious case, they do not necessarily prevent overcharging (i.e., filing more charges than he or she intends to prove in order to obtain a favorable plea.) Nor do they prevent targeting investigative resources to serve lawyers' own agendas. Monroe Freedman criticizes both practices. In his view, overcharging impairs a defendant's constitutional rights through "duress and trickery;" pursuing offenders rather than offenses is antithetical to "the rule of law." As an example, he cites Teamsters' Union leader Jimmy Hoffa, who was a "marked man from the day he told Robert Kennedy that he was nothing but a rich man's kid who had never had to earn a nickel in his life."[7] Students may need to be reminded that the Jimmy Hoffa in question was the Teamsters' infamous leader during the 1960s, not James Hoffa, Jr., a subsequent Teamsters' president.

---

[6] John Kaplan, "The Prosecutorial Discretion--A Comment," 60 *Nw. U.L. Rev.* 174, 180 (1965).

[7] Monroe Freedman, *Lawyers' Ethics in an Adversary System* 83, 88 (1975).

Similar challenges have been raised about IRS enforcement practices. The complexity and ambiguity of tax law creates many opportunities for inconsistent and unreasonable enforcement.[8]

It is interesting to ask for students' responses to these critiques. As a practical matter, how often could a defendant prove that illicit motivations were responsible for prosecution? Assuming that Freedman is right about the origin of James Hoffa's trials, could not Kennedy and his staff assert (and perhaps convince themselves) that concerns about corruption were their dominant considerations? Similarly, except in extreme cases, it would be difficult to establish that a prosecutor has offered a defendant special treatment because of feelings about defense counsel. However, these problems of proof are by no means unique, and commentators such as Gifford and Frase make strong arguments for more searching internal or external review of prosecutorial discretion.

The problem of racially selective prosecution is also likely to spark a good class discussion. As an overview on "Racially Based Selective Prosecution Jurisprudence" in 19 *Harvard Blackletter Law Journal* 140 (2003) suggests, there are often prudential, even if unconscious, motives for a prosecutor to target minorities. They are less likely to be able to afford counsel, which means that it will be easier to secure quick convictions. Racial bias among jurors will also facilitate conviction, and similar bias within the general public will place prosecutors under greater political pressure to bring cases against minorities, particularly where their victims are white. Given the difficulties of proving discriminatory intent under current standards, students can focus on what strategies might increase the perception and reality of equal justice within the criminal system. For other discussion of prosecutorial accountability including questions

---

[8] See John M. Broder, "Demonizing the I.R.S.: Is an Overview Needed or Just Less Posturing?," *N.Y. Times*, Sep. 20, 1997, at 1.

concerning sentencing discretion and targeting of drug crimes with racially disproportionate consequences, see the symposium in 68 *Fordham L. Rev.* (2000). For an example of sentencing issues, see Kevin C. McMunigal, "Are Prosecutorial Ethics Standards Different?," 68 *Fordham L. Rev.* 1453, 1469 (2000) (raising questions about whether a prosecutor should propose a harsher sentence than she thinks appropriate if she believes that a court might, but will not necessarily, "split the difference" between her request and that of defense counsel). For an overview of fairness issues, see Fred C. Zacharias, Justice in Plea Bargaining," 39 *William and Mary L. Rev.* 1121 (1998).

Problem 7c is based on the widely publicized Duke case in which the prosecutor was eventually disbarred. There was extensive media coverage, some of which make for entertaining class discussion, although the facts of the case were so extreme that it is hard to get much of a debate.

Problem 8

This problem is based on a real case. The heart of this problem lies in the dilemma that the prosecutor knows with near-100% certainty that either Harris or Adams killed Officer Wood, but has only a 50-50 guess as to which one was the guilty party. Discussion should center on whether this is enough to justify proceeding. The high public profile of the case pressures the prosecutor to obtain a conviction and, indeed, the death penalty. Thus, the statutory prohibition on seeking a death sentence for a juvenile, coupled with Harris's age and relative attractiveness, make Adams a more expedient target. But it is worth asking the class whether such extraneous factors can legitimately play a role in the decision about who to prosecute, even as a "tie-breaker." In that case, the prosecutor will be compelled merely to follow a hunch. One provocative question for discussion is whether the social value of convicting someone in this case outweighs the risk of convicting the wrong person – a real-life version of a case usually found only in hypothetical arguments about utilitarianism. A teacher can graphically suggest to students the practical impossibility of "playing it ethically safe" by releasing both Harris and Adams: How would you tell the press that you have just released two men, one of whom almost certainly murdered Officer Wood?

The problem is also meant to explore ABA Standard 3-3.9(a) (page 362). The standard's two sentences invoke quite different standards of certainty for proceeding with the prosecution. The first uses a probable cause standard, while the second speaks of "sufficient admissible evidence to support a conviction," which seems on its face to mean enough admissible evidence to prove guilt beyond a reasonable doubt. Part of the discussion of the problem could focus on the explanation for this double standard, and students should be pressed to explain why a prosecutor might proceed with a case lacking sufficient admissible evidence to support a conviction. Why should Standard 3-1.1(e) create a category of behavior that is permitted, but that the honorable prosecutor does not engage in? Presumably, the answer is that split-level standards such as 3.9 represent political compromises. In this case, an earlier version of the ABA Standards had described charging without probable cause as "unprofessional conduct," that is, conduct for which a prosecutor can be disciplined under prevailing rules. However, charging with insufficient evidence to support a conviction was described merely as something a prosecutor "should not" do. In effect, the first sentence was like a DR, while the second was akin to an EC. In the current version of the ABA Standards, however, the distinction between mandatory and precatory standards was eliminated, and Standard 3.9(a) was redrafted accordingly. Apparently, the redrafters could not agree on which sentence represented the better standard, and as a result they included both of them.

In our experience, most students will deny that their own subjective sense of whether the defendant is guilty has any relevance to their decision to prosecute, even in a death penalty case. Their typical argument is that such considerations are for the judge and jury to decide. A good follow-up inquiry is whether their answer would change if they were negotiating a plea agreement, in which judge and jury play no role. Another response is to ask students how their answer is consistent with Standard 3-1.2(c): "The duty of the prosecutor is to seek justice, not merely to convict." And a third follow-up is to point out that since prosecutors bring only a fraction of the cases they could, such discretionary judgments are a frequent and inevitable part of the job. The question, then, is whether they should exercise discretion based on which cases they can win or on which cases they think represent actual guilt. If the former, then they are back in the position of charging Adams because he will be easier to convict than Harris – the very position that most students will have rejected earlier.

Clips from the documentary film *The Thin Blue Line* are well worth showing if time permits. The problem should be discussed first, however, because it does not include facts included in the film. These facts make it quite clear that Harris rather than Adams was the murderer. Indeed, Harris –then on death row for a later murder – subsequently admitted that he killed Officer Wood. The present problem, by contrast, is meant to leave this ambiguous: on the one hand, Harris and not Adams has a motive for the shooting, and a criminal record; on the other, the unwillingness of Adams's brother to corroborate his alibi is highly suspicious.

The film also details several egregious prosecutorial abuses, which are enumerated in the Texas Court of Criminal Appeals decision that eventually freed Randall Adams after eleven years in prison, when the film drew national attention to his case. *Ex parte Adams*, 768 S.W.2d 281 (Tex.Cr.App. 1989). The prosecutor (Douglas "Mad Dog" Mulder, who at the time of the Adams case had never lost a criminal case) had:

• made a secret deal with David Harris to drop seven pending criminal charges in exchange for his testimony against Adams;

• told Harris to deny that he had made such a deal if he was asked;

• surprised the defense at trial with several eyewitnesses who identified Adams as the shooter, concealing that (a) two of the witnesses were being paid for their testimony, (b) the prosecutor had agreed to drop pending charges against these two witnesses and their daughter in exchange for the testimony, (c) the witnesses had originally picked the wrong man out of a lineup, only to be told by police who the "right" man (Adams) was;

- prevented the recall of these witnesses for further defense examination by falsely stating that they had moved to Illinois and that he did not have their address.

None of this behavior ever resulted in professional discipline. Mulder went on to practice as a criminal defense lawyer.

Initially, Adams was sentenced to death. The sentence was upheld by the Texas Court of Criminal Appeals, *Adams v. State*, 577 S.W.2d 717 (Tex.Cr.App. 1979). It was reversed by the U. S. Supreme Court, *Adams v. Texas*, 448 U.S. 38 (1980) on the ground that the Texas death penalty statute violated *Witherspoon v. Illinois*, 391 U.S. 510 (1968). At the prosecutor's request, the governor of Texas commuted Adams's sentence to life imprisonment, thereby avoiding a retrial.

Other questions that can spark a good class discussion involve prosecutorial policies such as the "no drop rule" described in Question 9, p 373. Some studies find that mandatory policies are helpful in forcing the criminal justice system to take domestic violence seriously, in deterring future abuse, and in minimizing victims' vulnerability to pressure and retaliation by taking the decision to proceed out of their hands By contrast, other researchers find little deterrent effect, increased risks of retaliation, and increased likelihood that victims will fail to call the police or seek needed services. Critics also worry that disregarding victims' own assessments of the risks and benefits of legal intervention victimizes them again, by compounding their trauma and further eroding their sense of efficacy and self esteem.[9]

Another issue of prosecutorial conduct involve deception. Steven Lubet's *The Importance of Being Honest* describes a case in which William "Cody" Neal called a Colorado sheriff's office on his cell phone and confessed that he had tortured and murdered three women and raped a forth. After several hours of negotiation, Neal said that he would turn himself in, but only if he could first speak to a defense attorney or a public defender. Instead of honoring the request, the

---

[9] Katherine T. Bartlett & Deborah Rhode, Gender and Law: Theory, Doctrine and Policy 491-95 (4th Ed., 2006).

office turned to Mark Pautler, the chief deputy district attorney, who agreed to impersonate a public defender. Afer the DA promised Neal access to a telephone and cigarettes, he turned himself in and was subsequently convicted and sentenced to death. Colorado's Attorney Regulation Counsel then charged Pautler with violating state ethics rules prohibiting conduct involving "dishonesty, fraud, deceit, or misrepresentation. Pautler was unapologetic, and told the disciplinary panel that he would make the same decision again to "save lives and take a killer off the street." Id., at 66. A divided board found that he committed misconduct, placed him on probation for a year and required him to take a twenty-hour course in legal ethics. The Colorado Supreme Court upheld that judgment. Matter of Pautler, 47 P.23d 1175 (2002). Lubet concludes that Pautler was "wrong, but not wrong enough to deserve formal punishment. The judicial system absolutely depends on lawyers telling the truth." Lubet, supra, at 66.

Another case that could spark class discussion is that of Daniel Bibb, a Manhattan prosecutor who threw a case because his supervisor insisted that he defend a position he believed was wrong. The case involved two defendants convicted of 1990 shooting of a bouncer outside the Palladium nightclub. When new evidence called their convictions into doubt, Bibb led the reinvestigation. He became convinced that the men were innocent. Manhattan District Attorney Robert Morgenthau was up for re-election and had been criticized by his opponent for trying the wrong men. Top officials in the office decided that Bibb's should contest the defendants' request for their convictions to be overturned. He did so, but in a manner calculated to help the defendants prevail. He tracked down hard to locate or reluctant witnesses and urged them to testify for the defense. He talked strategy with opposing counsel. "I did the best I could to lose," he acknowledged. He was successful. At the end of the hearing, Bibb's supervisors agreed to ask the judge to overturn the conviction of one defendant. He did so, and ordered a new trial to the other, who was subsequently acquitted.[10] Bibb resigned and is beginning his career again as a defense attorney.

---

[10] Benjamin Weiser, "Doubting Case, a Prosecutor Helped the Defense," N.Y. Times, June 23, 2008.

In a blog on Balkanization, Luban took issue with Stephen Giller's claim that Bibb could be subject to discipline because he was "entitled to his conscience but his conscience does not entitle him to subvert his client's case." In Giller's view, Bibb should have withdrawn or quit. Bibb declined to do so because he was concerned that another prosecutor might win, and two innocent men might have remained in prison. Luban argued that Bibb "deserves a medal, not a reprimand," because the "job of a prosecutor is to seek justice, not victory." David Luban, "When a Good Prosecutor Throws a Case," http://balkin.blogspot.com/2008/06/when-good-prosecutor-throws-case.html., (June 24, 2008). The thread of comments to this post give an overview of all sides of the debate. Discussing the Bibb case also offers professors an opportunity to introduce the recently-introduced MR 3.8(g) and (h).

Problem 9

The *Jones* decision on which Problem 9a is modeled is a good vehicle for discussing evidentiary practices. Inconsistencies in the *Jones* court's reasoning are worth exploring. If the witness' unavailability is not evidence subject to disclosure, why should it matter whether the defendant claims innocence?

In discussing prosecutors' disclosure practices, one additional issue to raise concerns disclosure of exculpatory evidence to a grand jury. According to the Comment to Model Rule 3.8, a grand jury counts as an *ex parte* proceeding in the sense of Model Rule 3.3(d), and thus requires prosecutors to disclose adverse material facts. The Duke rape case is a classic illustration of the injustices that can occur when evidence is withheld.

In discussing **Problem 10,** teachers should focus on ABA Model Rule 3.6. The (original) O. J. Simpson case provides an excellent vehicle for discussing the drawbacks of permitting attorneys to try cases in the press. One good example is prosecutor Marcia Clark's release of tapes of Nicole Simpson's 911 calls, well in advance of any ruling that they would be admissible as evidence. Given the overwhelming difficulties of impaneling a totally impartial jury in such a case, teachers may wish to discuss the advisability of judicial gag orders on attorneys in high profile proceedings.[11]

Problem 11

Other examples of trial conduct offer opportunities to explore the tension between prosecutors' dual obligations as advocates and ministers of justice. In a well-known article, Whitney North Seymour once maintained that the obligation to seek justice applies primarily to the decision to prosecute, and that once the trial arrives, the prosecutor's role becomes that of a "full-fledged fighting advocate."[12] As a description of prosecutorial practices the statement may be accurate, but as a normative proposition, its reasoning is problematic and worth exploring in light of the conduct in Problem 11. The results in the cited cases are as follows:

1) Baranyai:
Conviction reversed (inappropriate characterization).

2) Ortiz:
Conviction upheld (invited comment).

---

[11] For a general analysis, see Mawiyah Hooker & Elizabeth Lange, Note, "Limiting Extrajudicial Speech in High Profile Cases: The Duty of the Prosecutorial Speech in High Profile Cases: The Duty of the Prosecutor and Defense Attorney in Their Pre-Trial Communications with the Media," 16 *Geo. J. Leg. Ethics* 655 (2003).

[12] Whitney North Seymour, "Why Prosecutors Act Like Prosecutors," 11 *Rec. Assn. B. City of N. Y.* 302, 312-13 (1956).

3) <u>Johnson</u>:
Conviction reversed.

4) <u>Smith</u>:
Conviction sustained (comment was fair attempt by prosecutor to attack the credibility of the witness's statements).

5) <u>Scriptures</u>:
Conviction reversed in *Carruthers v. State* (because prosecutor "urge[d] the jury to follow the religious mandates of the Bible rather than Georgia law").[13]

6) <u>Cargle</u>
Prosecutors' statement impermissible and contributed to cumulative error .

7) <u>Blue jeans</u>:
Permitted, according to a newspaper account.

8) <u>Hernandez</u>:
Conviction sustained (prosecutor's race-neutral explanation for striking the jurors sufficed to overcome equal protection challenge).

The issue of peremptory challenges will often provoke excellent discussion. Many practitioners believe that *Batson* and *JEB* are widely violated by both prosecutors and defense attorneys. Part of the problem is that establishing pretext is extremely difficult. But a deeper difficulty is that lawyers often believe that they have no choice but to

---

[13] According to the prosecutor in *Carruthers*, "It's a sad day when a jury cannot be reminded of the importance of no Bible and its teachings," "Use of Scripture Leads to Reversal," *Nat'l L. J.* March 20, 2000, at A6 (quoting D. Brandon Hornsby).

use group characteristics as a proxy for attitudes. A line from the movie *Runaway Jury* is revealing; when asked "is there even such a thing as an objective jury?" a juror consultant responds, "not if I can help it." Ample empirical evidence suggests that jurors are unable or unwilling to reveal biases on voir dire. Many individuals are unaware of the extent of their own prejudices or are inclined to give answers consistent with what is expected of them (impartiality) rather than what they honestly believe.

Analysis of prosecutors' trial conduct and disclosure obligations can also raise issues involving incompetent adversaries. Commentators generally agree that constitutional rulings and bar disciplinary processes offer defendants grossly inadequate protection from ineffective assistance of counsel, particularly when it occurs at the pretrial stage. Students should consider whether the "seek justice" maxim imposes special obligations on prosecutors to compensate for defects in the adversarial process. For example, should prosecutors have an obligation to bring issues of competence to the court's attention? Could disciplinary agencies do more to encourage reporting (for example by providing anonymity for complainants)? Should bar organizations do more to improve the performance of court-appointed counsel through pro bono assistance and well-supported lobbying campaigns for indigent defense funding? What other strategies might be effective? Asking students who will never practice criminal law to focus on these issues may help build the awareness necessary for significant change.

CHAPTER VII: ETHICS IN ORGANIZATIONAL SETTINGS

A. Corporate Counseling and Whistleblowing

1. Introduction and
2. Cost/Benefit Frameworks

These materials, especially the Ford Pinto case, can generate exceptionally good classroom debate. Since some students respond with instinctive abhorrence to the concept of placing price tags on human life, it is useful to point out the vast range of contexts in which some implicit or explicit calculation is made. For example, every time highway administrators decide not to construct an overpass for train tracks, they can predict with some statistical certainty the number of injuries and deaths that will result. The *National Law Journal* article by Lavalle, though dated, is still relevant. It makes clear that both government regulators and those subject to regulation must inevitably make cost/safety tradeoffs, and that estimates of the value of life vary enormously. A more recent *New York Times* article notes that estimates of the value of life based on what individuals are willing to pay for safety range from $598,000 for airbags, $628,00 for smoke detectors and $4.1 million for other auto safety features, and $6 million for top grade tires. The military death benefits paid to a family of a Iraq soldier with three children would average $1. 9 million.[1]

A question worth exploring is how best to analyze the problem of trading off cost and safety. How explicit and consistent do we want valuations of human life to be, and what procedural and substantive criteria should guide analysis? Some students respond to the Pinto case by shifting responsibility from Ford executives and lawyers to the consumer or to government regulators. In response, it is useful to detail the usual problems of market failure: for example, the public's difficulty in assimilating all necessary information about all safety

---

[1] Bill Marsh, "Putting a Price on the Priceless: One Life," *N.Y. Times*, Sept. 9, 2007, at E4.

features of models; consumers' reluctance to contemplate the possibility of accidents when making purchase decisions; the effects on nonpurchasers who will ride in cars or whose lives would be materially diminished by the purchaser's death, etc. Comparable inadequacies arise from regulatory solutions. Often the industry has better data than regulators on safety risks or is able to gain concessions through intensive lobbying, as happened in the Ford Pinto case.

That case is also a good opportunity for exploring different methods of moral argument. Most of the limits of utilitarianism that MacIntyre describes in the cited study emerge clearly in Ford's decisionmaking. As MacIntyre's essay indicates, managers' seemingly straightforward cost/benefit calculation rested on certain non-utilitarian and problematic assumptions about:

1)   which alternative to use in measuring safety costs (why $11 rather than $5?);

2)   which method and figures to use in valuing human life; and

3)   what long-term consequences to take into account as a result of lives lost (note that Ford excluded from consideration the costs to third parties, such as families of victims, and the effects of adverse publicity on company reputation, recruitment, morale, and sales).

A subtle but important point is that each method of assigning a dollar value to human life incorporates an implicit judgment about whose values count. Thus:

Pricing human life by loss to dependents implicitly privileges values of dependents.

Pricing human life by willingness-to-pay implicitly privileges the values of the one facing risks.

Pricing human life by looking at the tradeoffs that existing laws and policies implicitly prioritizes legislative or judicial value.

Pricing human life by looking at lost income implicitly adopts a framework based on social wealth.

Beneath the seemingly-scientific, seemingly-value-neutral, seemingly-rational and impersonal techniques of cost/benefit analysis lie a host of value judgments and assumptions that are often unexamined.

But if, as the passages quoted from Jackall suggest, the language of costs and benefits is the only language that business executive feel "comfortable" with, then the lawyer's counseling problem may be to speak to the client in "cost/benefit-ese" regardless of whether it is the most ethically satisfying vocabulary. In much the same way, a lawyer counseling a client with strong religious convictions may do the best job by using Biblical language, whether the lawyer shares the client's religion or not. This is a question to raise with students: Is the best maxim for the lawyer-as-counselor "When in Rome, speak as the Romans do"?

B. Sarbanes-Oxley

This chapter's discussion of corporate lawyers' whistleblowing responsibilities takes as its chief example the Sarbanes-Oxley reporting requirements, together with the modifications in Model Rule 1.13 that followed Sarbanes-Oxley. For easy reference, we have reprinted relevant portions of the SEC's regulations implementing the Act's mandate in Section 307. The Notes and Questions on pp. 420-23 provide the needed roadmap to § 205, and they, together with Problem 2, should form the centerpiece of discussion. Because these notes explain the meaning of § 205 provisions, professors need not assign students to read the actual regulation; instead, they can simply refer back to it when they work through the notes and questions.

Problem 2(a) is an exercise in construing the language of § 205. The fact situation is drawn from the Enron case, as discussed in the Bankruptcy Examiner's lengthy report. It is unnecessary for students to grasp the distinction between a true sale letter and a true issuance letter. (According to Neal Batson, the bankruptcy examiner, some of Enron's lawyers did not understand it even while writing the letters.) All they have to understand from the facts is that the lawyer believes that the deal as the client wishes to structure it is not permissible. The question is what the lawyer should do about it, and the key piece of § 205 is § 205.2(e). This is the notoriously opaque definition of "evidence of a material violation." This must be "credible evidence, based upon which it would be unreasonable, under the circumstances, for a prudent and competent attorney not to conclude that it is reasonably likely that a material violation has occurred, is ongoing, or is about to occur...." The exercise for the student is how to untie the linguistic knot. The key lies in Note 3, page 421. As it suggests, if even one prudent and competent lawyer in a firm believes there is no credible evidence of a material violation, no reporting obligation would exist. For then one must assume that this prudent and competent lawyer will not reasonably conclude that a material violation is reasonably likely. Thus, in Problem 2, the associate confronts an experienced supervising partner who believes – reasonably, one must assume – that there is nothing improper in the deal. It follows that there is no evidence of a material violation, as defined in § 205.2(e), and thus no up-the-ladder reporting obligation.

However, the newly amended version of Rule 1.13(b) states that if the deal is likely to do substantial harm to the corporate client, "the lawyer *shall* refer the matter [up the ladder]" (emphasis added). So Model Rule 1.13(b) apparently requires up the ladder reporting even where Sarbanes-Oxley does not.

Model Rule 5.2(a) states that the associate remains bound by Rule 1.13(b) even if directed to the contrary by the supervisor. Rule 5.2(b) creates an exception if the supervisory lawyer has a "reasonable resolution of an arguable question of professional duty," but here the problem stipulates that the associate is convinced that "it is not even a close call that the transactions are illegal." It *may* be arguable that the illegal deals are unlikely to harm the client, in which case the exception applies. But otherwise, Rule 5.2(a) requires the associate to report up the ladder even if his or her supervisor forbids it.

Problem 2b Here the operative clause of § 205 is § 205.3(b)(3). The question is whether two weeks is a reasonable time for the chief legal officer to respond to the report. We think the answer is yes – in which case the associate is obligated to go over the CLO's head to the audit committee or other relevant committee of the board of directors, or to the board as a whole.

Problem 2c This is a vexed question currently being debated, as explained in Note 5, page 422. Do SEC regulations pre-empt state ethics requirements? The Washington and California bars say no, but Supreme Court preemption doctrine is inconsistent. Under the *Rice* standard quoted on page 422, the presumption is that federal law does not preempt state ethics rules, because these lie within the "historic police powers" of the states. The exception is when preemption is "the clear and manifest purpose of Congress." Here, one might argue that Congress clearly and manifestly intended to regulate the conduct of lawyers. However, the federal regulation merely permits, not requires, lawyers to reveal client confidences in order to prevent fraud or rectify fraud. Thus, a lawyer might argue that since the state regulations forbid revelation of confidences and the federal regulation does not require revelation, the lawyer can comply with both by not revealing – and, furthermore, that the state may therefore discipline the lawyer for revealing confidences. That raises a question: does a federal law permitting revelation of confidences preclude a state from disciplining a lawyer who chooses to reveal? We do not suggest that there is a definitive answer to this question.

C. In-House Counsel

The centerpiece for discussion in this section should be Problem 3, which refers to the exceptionally readable and interesting selection from Robert Jackall's *Moral Mazes.* The Hewlett Packard case provides an ideal opportunity for role simulations; students can take the parts of Hurd, Baskins, Dunn, Hunsaker, Perkins, Sonsini, and congressional representatives who questioned them at subsequent hearings.

D. Supervisory and Subordinate Lawyers

The Berkey-Kodak case is an excellent case study for raising questions about the relations between bureaucratic structures, individual responsibilities, and disciplinary norms. If time permits, many students would be interested in reading the longer narratives cited in the section's bibliographic references. They will also want to know what became of Fortenberry. After he left Donovan, Leisure, he went to work for the Antitrust Division of the Justice Department, where he remained until his death in February, 1987.

Appropriate disciplinary action can be discussed in connection with materials in Chapter XV, which raise the question of individual versus general deterrence. In determining sanctions, should the controlling issue be protection of the public? If so, then the disbarment of Perkins hardly seems necessary. Alternatively, should bar disciplinary committees give greater weight to the *in terrorem* and expressive functions of punishment? If lying to the court under oath doesn't warrant the profession's most severe sanctions, what does? Does leniency for a Wall Street partner reflect a compassionate judgment that he has been punished enough or a double standard of justice for the bar's elite and non-elite attorneys? Fortenberry's conduct raises similar questions, which lend themselves to role-playing. Students can place themselves in his position, or in the positions of Donovan Leisure lawyers evaluating him for partnership prospects, bar disciplinary committee members considering sanctions, or Justice Department officials reviewing his job application.

Question 6, p. 445. This question asks about New York's version of DR 1-102(a), which makes law firms as well as individual lawyers liable for discipline. It is important to realize that this provision has almost never been invoked against law firms (as opposed to individual lawyers), and to date has never been invoked against any large law firm. It may be useful to ask students about the circumstances under which it should be invoked, and what accounts for its lack of implementation.

The chapter concludes with materials that can put the Berkey-Kodak problem in broader context: from C. S. Lewis's justly famous speech "The Inner Ring," Patrick Schiltz's now-well-known article on large law-firm practice, and David Luban's essay on the Milgram experiments and the Berkey-Kodak case. The point of these excerpts is straightforward: all of them emphasize that in real life, unlike Dante's *Divine Comedy*, the road to perdition does not have a sign advising "Abandon all hope ye who enter here!" Instead, lawyers drift into unethical behavior one micro-step at a time, often, as Schiltz notes, without even noticing that they are drifting away from "the notions of right and wrong by which you conduct your personal life." Many students will know something about the Milgram experiments, but probably not the details, and it is worth exploring Milgram's incredible finding that "[t]wo out of three people you pass in the street would electrocute you if a laboratory technician ordered them to." The Lewis essay has a slightly different point. His emphasis is not so much the incremental nature of The Fall. Rather, his point is that the real motivation is likely to be something other than greed or callousness – it is likely to be the desire to belong to the Inner Ring – a term for what Americans call the "inner circle" or (in high school) the "in crowd." The point is worth dwelling on, as are the final two sentences of Lewis's piece, which beautifully remind us that when he talks about becoming a scoundrel, Lewis is talking about something that may contribute to worldly success as well as failure and disgrace.

Schiltz's paper was originally published as the centerpiece of a *Vanderbilt Law Review* symposium, with replies by leading practitioners and scholars and a rejoinder by Schiltz. Professors may wish to consult the rest of the symposium in preparing to teach this unit; Chapter 2 (on the conditions of practice) in Rhode's *In the Interests of Justice*; or the recent symposium, "Perspectives on on Lawyer Happiness," in 58 *Syracuse L. Rev.* 217 (2008).

CHAPTER VIII: NEGOTIATION AND MEDIATION

This chapter begins with a negotiating exercise that students must perform outside of class. It will be necessary, therefore, to give the assignment, pair students off, and distribute instructions in advance of the class (we suggest a week in advance). Professors should pair students off and instruct them to follow the rules for both sides set out in the casebook. The professor should then distribute the following instructions so that students receive only the special instructions for the side that they are representing. Some instructors videotape the negotiations of one or more pairs of student volunteers and use selections from the videotapes in class; others videotape volunteer lawyers. Here we provide full instructions for both plaintiffs' and defendant's attorneys, on separate pages for ease in photocopying.

Professors who have used the Valdez negotiation case in the past should note that our exercise changes some of the facts from earlier versions. Most importantly, in our problem, it is the plaintiff, rather than a defense witness, who "remembers" a fact that he had denied in his deposition. Secondly, because the defendant is self-insured, no conflict-of-interest problems arise from the subrogation of the defense by an insurer. Third, though the plaintiff's lawyer labors under the mistaken belief that the jurisdiction's law is contributory rather than comparative negligence, we stipulate that the Valdezes' failure to fasten Rickie's seat belt is not an absolute bar to recovery.

Between 1979 and 1982, Steven D. Pepe used an earlier version of the Valdez problem in role-plays and surveys involving 1034 litigation attorneys in Michigan, together with a national sample of 1513 large firm litigators, 256 state judges, 75 federal judges, and 128 law professors.[1]

---

[1] Steven D. Pepe, *Standards of Legal Negotiations -- Summary of Preliminary Findings* (unpublished 1983). Pepe presented separate statistics for the national sample and the Michigan sample, which we consolidate here for convenience.

Pepe's findings on the central issues in the exercise are as follows:

1. Must a lawyer disclose a client's false deposition testimony? 56% of the total sample said no. Of the litigators, however, 72% said no.

2. May a lawyer enter into a settlement without disclosing false deposition testimony? 39% of the litigators said yes.

3. If asked during negotiations about the portion of the deposition testimony now known to be false, how should the lawyer respond? Just under half (47%) responded that the answer must be truthful and complete. 50% of the litigators stated that they could give a partially true but incomplete answer provided that it does not reveal the element of the deposition that is false.

4. May (or must) the defense attorney use the plaintiff's sense of guilt and anguish as a negotiating lever in obtaining a more favorable settlement? Over 84% of the attorneys believed the attorney *may*, and about half thought the defense attorney *must*, appeal to the plaintiff's guilt if it seems that doing so would lead to a more advantageous settlement; 18% of the national sample and 25% of the Michigan sample stated that they would not make such an appeal even if it was an effective tactic. A substantially higher number of the federal judges, 46%, stated that they would not do so even if it was permissible.

5. What should the defense lawyer do with the knowledge of the Valdezes' undocumented status? 55% of the lawyers thought it permissible to emphasize the risk of deportation as a negotiation tactic (38% disagreed). 49% stated that it is permissible for the defense lawyer to report the Valdezes to the immigration authorities (the Immigration and Customs Enforcement (ICE) division of the Department of Homeland Security) and disclose having done so prior to negotiating the settlement. However, only 16% believed it proper for the attorney to use the threat of deportation as a negotiation tool. And 36% believed that it is permissible to say that their client is likely to report the plaintiffs to the ICE.

VALDEZ v. ACE AUTO REPAIR
Confidential Instructions for the Defendant's Attorney

You are a partner in a large firm that represents Ace Auto Repair. The company has been sued in a wrongful death action brought on behalf of a couple, Dora and Frank Valdez, whose only child, a five-year-old boy nicknamed Rickie, was recently fatally injured in an automobile accident.[2] Ace owns a nationwide chain of auto repair shops. The company is self-insured for losses under $300,000; for claims above that amount, it carries excess liability insurance.

Plaintiffs have filed a complaint seeking recovery, according to proof at trial, of damages for medical and funeral expenses as well as additional damages for the parents' loss of society, services, and expected economic benefit from their son, as well as their emotional distress in witnessing the accident and Rickie's suffering.[3]

Here is what you know about the accident. About three months ago, Mr. Valdez entered a left bend in a rural road, apparently a bit fast. When he hit the brakes on his 1993 Chevy Citation, it veered to the right and Mr. Valdez lost control. The car went off the road and slammed sideways into a tree. The curve has a 25 m.p.h. speed reduction sign in

---

[2] This statutory wrongful death action is brought by the personal representative of the deceased for the spouse and next of kin (e.g., children and parents). The statute consolidates the claims of the survivors and decedent.

[3] In the state where you practice, in an action for the recovery of damages for personal injury, the amount of damages shall not be stated in the complaint.

an otherwise 55 m.p.h. road. Rickie was not wearing a seat belt and was severely injured. He was rushed to a nearby hospital where he drifted in and out of consciousness for four days, apparently suffering some pain. Despite all medical efforts, on the fifth day he lapsed into a coma and died several hours later. About all this, there is no dispute.

There is also no dispute as to why the brakes caused the swerve. Inspection after the accident showed brake fluid on the left front brake and brake shoes indicating a leak and loss of braking power in the left front wheel. In addition, the cylinder on the right front brake was sticking and inspection of that brake indicated that it locked up in the sudden application of the brake and aggravated the swerve to the right. It is not in dispute that two days before the accident, Mr. Valdez had taken the car for service to Ace Auto.

What is in dispute is whether on that occasion, Mr. Valdez had, as he claimed at his deposition, requested that Gene Rossini, a garage mechanic employed by the garage, "check the brakes." Mr. Valdez stated that he told the mechanic to fix the alignment because the car was pulling to the right, the steering wheel vibrated, and his tires were wearing unevenly. He also stated that he told Rossini to check the brakes because the pull to the right sometimes seemed worse when he applied the brakes.

Rossini has stated in a deposition that Valdez was complaining about the car pulling right, and that Valdez thought the alignment was off since the steering vibrated and his tires were wearing unevenly. He testified that Valdez never said anything about the pull to the right being worse when braking, nor did he ever ask Ace Auto to check the brakes. Valdez also asked for an engine tune-up and lube job, and in the process of the latter, they routinely "topped up" the brake fluid that cars lose through eventual evaporation. The car was severely out of alignment. After realignment and a tire rotation, the car was test driven, and drove smoothly and no problem was apparent. Rossini admitted that he did not test the brakes on the test drive, nor try a "panic stop," since he had no reason to do so. There was no sign of pulling during normal braking, though he admitted the fluid had just been topped up and that sticking brake cylinders are often intermittent. Rossini's deposition includes some inconsistencies about what Mr. Valdez told him to look for. These raise some doubts in your mind about Rossini's reliability, and about what kind of witness he would make at trial.

Last week, three months after the accident and four weeks after the depositions of Mr. Valdez and Mr. Rossini, plaintiffs' attorney called regarding some Interrogatories you have submitted. Plaintiffs' attorney is a solo practitioner whom you sense has little experience in negligence cases and who appears to have put little time in on the Valdez case. Once again you offered your condolences for the boy's death. Plaintiffs' attorney asked if you would like to meet to discuss the possibility of settlement. You agreed to meet him in your office. You emphasized that by meeting, your client is in no way admitting liability, but that it is company policy to talk about settlement whenever asked. In response to your question, plaintiffs' attorney confirmed that plaintiffs' actual damages to date were $9,500 for unpaid medical and funeral bills.

Here are a few other important aspects of the case as you prepare for the settlement meeting in your office:

1. Rossini testified that Dora Valdez came to see him right before the suit was filed and was crying. She seemed very unsteady and left yelling "It wasn't the seat belts; Rickie hated the belts. It was your brakes."

2. You think that the Valdezes may also have been negligent in a few respects.

First, although Valdez denied it in his deposition, you suspect that he went into the turn pretty fast and hit the brakes hard.

Second, your client has told you that given the type of brake failure that occurred, it is unlikely that after picking up his car Mr. Valdez would not have noticed that the brakes felt soft and still caused the car to pull to the right. If he did notice the pull to the right, then he should be considered negligent in continuing to drive the car without bringing the car back to Ace for further repairs. Again, however, Valdez has denied in his deposition noticing any problem with the brakes after leaving the repair shop.

Third, you also believe it likely that the child would have been far less severely injured (or not injured at all) if his parents had strapped him into a seat belt.[4]

3. Shortly before the accident, a new law went into effect that changed the law of contributory negligence. Under the old law, a jury would have been required (as a matter of law at least) to deny any recovery to the Valdezes if (1) they were found negligent and (2) negligence was a substantial factor causing the accident. Under the new standard, referred to as comparative negligence, the negligence of the plaintiffs and the defendant will be weighed against each other. The plaintiffs could still recover in part even if they were also found negligent; but their recovery would be diminished by the percentage of their comparative negligence. From something Valdez's attorney said in the phone conversation, you suspect that plaintiff's counsel is unaware of this change in the law.

---

[4] There is a mandatory seat belt law in effect which required Rickie to wear a seat belt when the car was in motion. Under the statute, a violation does not establish negligence as a matter of law, or negligence per se, but it constitutes evidence of negligence.

4. Through a private investigator that you employ, you are aware that the Valdezes are citizens of El Salvador. They are in this country as undocumented aliens and thus remain here illegally. You do not believe that they would be subject to criminal charges if caught, but you are certain that they could be deported in a civil proceeding.[5] You also believe it highly probable that the Valdezes would prefer to continue to reside in the United States. Your client, Ace Auto, doesn't know about the Valdezes' status; but Charles Simms, your contact at Ace, might inform federal immigration authorities if you told him that the Valdezes were here illegally.

If the case goes to trial and the jury believes that Rossini failed to check the brakes after Valdez asked him to do so, you suspect that a jury might make a substantial award to the Valdezes. Trial, however, would be a long time off: the court's trial docket is about three years behind. You have not taken any depositions of Mrs. Valdez or of their physician. Keeping discovery at a minimum has kept costs low, but has made your evaluation of the case more difficult.

There are many traditional "rules of thumb" in dealing with settlement figures for personal injury and property damage cases, but a wrongful death action is a different story. It is difficult to predict an award in this area should the case go to trial, but you feel it likely that if a jury finds Ace Auto Repair liable at all, and they might well do so if they

---

[5] An undocumented alien present in the United States is basically subject to criminal prosecution only if he or she reentered the country illegally after having been deported. A civil deportation proceeding is therefore the most likely consequence if the Valdezes are reported to the Immigration and Customs Enforcement (ICE) division of the Department of Homeland Security.

believe Mr. Valdez, the plaintiffs could recover well over $200,000. You are aware from *Jury Verdicts Weekly*, a publication reporting on recent judgments in your locale, that juries recently returned verdicts in similar circumstances in the amount of $200,000, in cases of no comparative negligence by the plaintiffs. You estimate that trying the case would cost Ace close to $10,000.

Apart from the arguments that you might make about the Valdezes' own negligence, the only factor that seems likely to lead to a lower jury award is the fact that the Valdezes are Salvadorans. According to reports of others, juries often give lower awards to members of minority groups. Finally, you think that Mrs. Valdez may feel guilty about not fastening her son's seat belt. She probably fears reliving it all at trial and running the risk that a jury may feel she was responsible for the death. You suspect that the tacit admission of fault by Ace Auto Repair in settling may make a settlement much more important to Mrs. Valdez than the amount of damages – particularly if she must face three years of uncertainty before obtaining a verdict.

In view of the risks of liability, your client has authorized you to settle now for up to $80,000, but you believe that the Valdezes might accept substantially less than that – and you have advised the client of your views.

You should try to reach a settlement in the time allotted.

VALDEZ v. ACE AUTO REPAIR

Confidential Instructions for the Plaintiffs' Attorney

You are a solo practitioner sharing office space and a secretary with two other solo practitioners. You have a general practice: real estate, probate, family law, workers' compensation, and criminal defense work. You have done some but not very much plaintiff's personal injury work. Your clients in this case are Dora and Frank Valdez, both citizens of El Salvador who have lived in the United States about a year.

About three months ago, while driving with their five-year-old son, Rickie, the Valdezes had an accident in their 1993 Chevy Citation. Mr. Valdez entered a left bend in a rural road, apparently a bit fast,. When he hit the brakes, the car veered to the right and Mr. Valdez lost control. The car went off the road and slammed sideways into a tree. The curve has a 25 m.p.h. speed reduction sign in an otherwise 55 m.p.h. road. Rickie was not wearing a seat belt and was severely injured. He was rushed to a nearby hospital where he drifted in and out of consciousness for four days, apparently suffering some pain. Despite all medical efforts, on the fifth day he lapsed into a coma and died several hours later. About all this, there is no dispute.

There is also no dispute as to why the brakes caused the swerve. Inspection after the accident showed brake fluid on the left front brake and brake shoes indicating a leak and loss of braking power in the left front wheel. In addition, the cylinder on the right front brake was sticking and inspection of that brake indicated that it locked up in the sudden application of the brake and aggravated the swerve to the right. It is not in dispute that two days before the accident, Mr. Valdez had taken the car for service to Ace Auto.

In addition to the horror of losing their only son, the Valdezes face $9,500 in unpaid medical and funeral bills. They came to see you a few months ago and you promptly filed a wrongful death suit on their behalf against Ace Auto Repair, where Mr. Valdez had taken the car for servicing two days before the accident.[1] Ace Auto owns a national chain

---

[1] This statutory wrongful death action is brought by the personal

of garages.

---

representative of the deceased for the spouse and next of kin (e.g., children and parents). The Statute consolidates the claims of the survivors and decedent.

The Complaint seeks recovery, according to proof at trial, of the damages for medical and funeral expenses as well as additional damages for the parents' loss of society, services, and expected economic benefit from their son, as well as their emotional distress in witnessing the accident and Rickie's suffering.[2] You believe that if the jury finds no contributory negligence by the plaintiffs, it could return an award as high as $200,000.

Mr. Valdez claimed at his deposition that he asked the Ace garage mechanic to "check the brakes." He stated that he told the mechanic that the car was pulling to the right, that the steering wheel vibrated, that the tires were wearing unevenly, and that the car needed realignment. He also stated that the pull to the right was sometimes worse when applying the brakes and that he mentioned this to the mechanic when he told him to "check the brakes."

The mechanic, Gene Rossini, stated in a deposition that Valdez was complaining about the car pulling to the right, and that Valdez thought the alignment was off since the steering wheel vibrated and his tires were wearing unevenly. At his deposition, Rossini says that he does not recall Valdez saying anything about the pull to the right when braking, and he denies that Valdez ever asked him to check the brakes. Valdez did ask for an engine tune-up and lube job, and in the process of the latter, Ace routinely "topped up" the brake fluid that cars lose through eventual evaporation. The car was severely out of alignment. After realignment and a tire rotation, the car was test driven, and drove smoothly and no problem was apparent. Rossini further stated that he did not test the brakes on the test drive, nor try a "panic stop," because he had no reason to do so. There was no sign of pulling during normal braking, though he admitted the fluid had just been topped up and that sticking brake cylinders are often intermittent.

In looking over Rossini's deposition, you found some inconsistencies concerning what Rossini says that Mr. Valdez told him to

---

[2] In the state where you practice, in an action for the recovery of damages for personal injury, the amount of damages shall not be stated in the complaint.

look for. You could depose Rossini again, a process that would be expensive, especially since the defendant would surely resist a second deposition.

If jurors believe Rossini, it will be difficult to prove negligence. You are also worried that the defendant will be able to claim successfully that the Valdezes were guilty of contributory negligence, thus barring their right to any recovery in the case. The boy's own physician believes the accident would not have been fatal, or even particularly serious, if the child had been buckled in. You believe that the failure of the Valdezes to fasten their son's seat belt will not constitute contributory negligence as a matter of law, but will be a question for the jury.[3]

There is another way in which you fear that the Valdezes may have been contributorily negligent. Mr. Valdez testified at his deposition that he did not recall noticing any problem with the brakes after he left the repair shop. Since giving his deposition, Mr. Valdez has admitted to you that he now "remembers" that the brakes "still seemed weak" to him after the tune-up. Indeed, while the car was now driving smoothly, he noticed that when he applied the brakes, it still pulled to the right. He intended to take the car back to Ace to complain, but he hadn't gotten around to doing so. You are certain Ace's lawyers don't know about Mr. Valdez's change in recollection.

Also, while Frank denied it at his deposition, Dora Valdez has told you privately that Frank was driving too fast and that she had told him to slow down. She asked you not to tell Frank that she told you this because it would make him angry.

Your final worry is that the Valdezes told you for the first time after

---

[3] There is a mandatory seat belt law in effect which required Rickie to wear a seat belt when the car was in motion. Under the statute, a violation does not establish negligence as a matter of law or negligence per se, but constitutes evidence of negligence.

you had filed the suit that they are undocumented aliens, and are residing in the United States illegally. The Valdezes entered the country legally on a visitor's visa to visit relatives. Thereafter, they decided to stay beyond the visa's expiration date. They were all the more interested in staying after Frank's uncle found him a job. You do not know whether Ace's attorney knows about your clients' undocumented status, but you fear that it is possible that it will be discovered before trial. In fact, you are aware that the opposing counsel is a member of a large firm which is known for its thorough, and consequently expensive, discovery practice before trial. You are worried that Ace or Ace's attorney might report them to the immigration authorities (the Immigration and Customs Enforcement (ICE) division of the Department of Homeland Security) or use the threat of reporting them as leverage in settlement negotiations.

The only really strong factor working in your favor is the imbalance between the parties. Unless a local jury would be ill-disposed toward Salvadorans, your clients are likely to be appealing because they are attractive, vulnerable, hard-working, and not well off. They are suing a "deep pocket," a corporation owning a nationwide chain of auto repair garages.

If you go to trial, there is a risk of a defense verdict and you would then never recover your ever-growing costs of trial preparation, let alone any fees for the time spent in the courtroom. On the other hand, there is always the possibility for a substantial verdict if you wait it out and go to trial. The wait might be quite long. The defendant has not yet taken a deposition of Dora Valdez or the doctor who treated Rickie. More significantly, the court's trial docket is about three years behind.

In short, you now view the prospects for the case somewhat dimly. The Valdezes have told you that they would rather recover nothing than be deported. They are also not at all eager to go to trial: the memories of the accident and five days thereafter are so shatteringly painful that they want to get all this behind them as swiftly as possible. You have not tried to persuade them otherwise. Dora Valdez is also feeling unreasonably guilty over her not fastening the seat belts. She wants to blame Ace Auto, but cannot.

The Valdezes told you that they would like to recover enough to cover their medical and funeral bills. You represent them on a contingency fee basis, which gives you 1/3 of the total recovery before trial, and 2/5 of any recovery after trial. Therefore, you would have to secure a settlement of at least $15,000 in order to recover their bills, to date, of $9,500, your 1/3 fee of $4750, and your own out-of-pocket costs of $750 for filing fees, deposition transcripts, and the like.[4]

You are about to meet at the office of defendant's attorney. You called opposing counsel regarding some Interrogatories that had been submitted, and asked if a meeting to discuss the case was of interest. You learned that Ace does not concede negligence, but that it is their policy to discuss settlement whenever asked. In response to their attorney's question, you confirmed that plaintiffs' actual damages to date were $9,500 for unpaid medical and funeral bills. In addition, you have learned in discovery that Ace is self-insured for losses up to $300,000; for claims above that amount, it carries excess liability insurance.

You should try to reach settlement in the time permitted.

***

_____

[4] Assume for this exercise that attorneys take their out-of-pocket expenses off the top of any settlement.

The text material provides enough legal background to discuss the principal issues in the Valdez negotiation concerning candor and disclosure. But it is worth adding some discussion of the defense lawyer's possible tactic of threatening to report the Valdezes to the immigration authorities, which may border on the felony of extortion. The Model Penal Code, in §223.4(4), "Theft by Extortion," provides that "A person is guilty of theft if he purposely obtains property of another by threatening to...cause an official to take or withhold action." Section 223.4 adds that "It is an affirmative defense...that the property obtained by threat of...invocation of official action was honestly claimed as restitution or indemnification for harm done to which such...official action relates, or as compensation for property or lawful services." The official comments explain that this affirmative defense "firmly establishes the intention not to intrude into what many regard as legitimate negotiating tactics."[5] Such considerations also influenced the decision by the drafters of the Model Rules not to include a provision comparable to DR 7-105(A) of the Code. That rule prohibits attempting to obtain advantage in civil cases by threatening criminal prosecution.

The defendant's threat to report the Valdezes to the immigration authorities is not part of a claim for restitution or indemnification, nor does the lawsuit relate to whatever official action the immigration authorities would take; in the present case, therefore, the affirmative defense is unavailable to the defense lawyer. A subsequent comment suggests that §223.4(4) is directed mostly at "extortion under color of office," but the comment adds that "the threat of an ordinary layman to file a criminal complaint or a civil suit based upon injuries

---

[5] 2 *Model Penal Code and Commentaries (Official Draft and Revised Comments)* 213 (1980). The specific reference of this sentence is to the tactic of threatening to accuse another of a crime in order to induce a favorable settlement of a civil claim, but the affirmative defense itself is broader, and includes extortion by threatening to bring about official action.

done him might be said to fall within paragraph (4)." Although a report to the immigration authorities is neither a criminal complaint nor a civil suit, these seem like illustrative examples, not an exclusive list, and the threat against the Valdezes falls naturally under the plain language of §223.4(4). A second question is whether compelling a favorable settlement from the Valdezes amounts to "obtaining property"; the answer is presumably yes, since the definition of "property" in §223.0(6) includes choses-in-action.

The text points out that comment *f* to Model Penal Code section 223.4 specifically exempts from the definition of extortion threatens to press criminal charges made during the negotiation of a civil case growing out of the same conduct. The reason is that it is simply too unrealistic to expect that a lawyer (or client) would discuss the settlement of a civil lawsuit without mentioning that the conduct is criminal. However, matters would stand differently if the lawyer threatened to report the adversary for an unrelated crime that the lawyer happened to know about, in order to force the adversary to settle a civil case. That may be extortion. And this latter case seems like a better analogy to threatening to report the Valdezes to the immigration authorities. Their status as undocumented aliens has nothing to do with their wrongful death suit or the accident.

Professors may wish to compare the Model Penal Code with their own jurisdiction's extortion statutes. Even if the class eventually concludes that threatening to report the Valdezes to the immigration authorities is not a case of extortion, students who have completed the exercise and either used the tactic or considered using it are usually quite perturbed to discover how close the question is. This serves two valuable functions. First, it is always useful to remind students that their conduct as lawyers is subject to the same legal standards that apply to everyone else. Many discussions of negotiation proceed in a legal vacuum, by assuming that whether or not to "play hardball" is simply up to the conscience of the negotiator. Second, for those students who find the threat of deportation morally objectionable, but fear that they are being excessively softhearted, it can be very helpful to point out that what they may think of as the moral equivalent of blackmail may well be blackmail in the legal sense as well.

The remaining material in the chapter is quite straightforward to teach. The custody example usually provokes a heated discussion. However, teachers should remain sensitive to the possibility that students in the class have experienced acrimonious custody battles first-hand, in either their own divorces or the divorces of their parents. Some of our own students have indicated that the topic is not an easy one for them.

Mediation

Many teachers may decide to omit this section, particularly if they devote only a single class to negotiation ethics. Others may wish to combine this material with Chapter XIII, Section F.3, on alternative dispute resolution. The combined readings on mediation and ADR can be covered in a single classroom hour.

In discussing evaluative versus facilitative mediation, it bears noting that some experts have argued that the process should also be "transformative"; the goal is to give parties greater understandings, new skills for problem-solving, and an enhanced sense of control.[6]

Problem 4.

One Missouri court's resolution of the disclosure issue is discussed in the Notes on p. 493. However, the court's assumptions – that the lawyer-mediator had breached his duties by failing to inquire fully into the husband's financial affairs or to advise the wife to litigate the issue – are controversial within the profession. Many mediators maintain that it is entirely improper to advise one of the parties to litigate, or to do independent investigation.

In analyzing this problem, a great deal turns on the retainer agreement with the couple, and what exactly was said to them and by them. The problem stipulates that "you were serving as a mediator rather than an advocate," but the crucial question is not whether you were functioning as an "advocate," but rather whether you had given either of them reason to believe that they were retaining you as a lawyer and establishing a client-lawyer relationship. If it was clear that no such relationship was formed (as it should have been if you did it right), then

---

[6]   Robert A. Baruch Bush & Joseph Folger, *The Promise of Mediation: Responding to Conflict Through Empowerment and Recognition* (1994).

120

your liability is probably nil. Your stance of neutrality and confidentiality – although it is not the only possible stance for a mediator to assume – is very much in the mainstream of the mediation profession.

CHAPTER IX: THE LAWYER'S COUNSELING ROLE

In this chapter we present counseling problems from disparate areas of the law: corporate practice, family practice, business and personal tax, and government lawyers (a discussion centering around the lawyers who wrote the well-known "torture memos"). Teachers who wish to spend only one or two classroom hours on counseling can choose the problems to suit their students' interests; this may be the opportunity to get the bored but dutiful future tax lawyer in the back row truly engaged in discussion. This is also a class well-suited to guest-teaching by a tax or family law colleague, or a panel discussion involving practitioners in the relevant fields. These problems are designed to be accessible to all law students, whether or not they have any familiarity with the substantive law. Many students with little substantive background in the fields find the ethical issues surprisingly interesting.

A. Corporate Practice

Professors who have taught Chapter VII, Section A may want to omit classroom discussion of Problem 1, since it covers much of the same ground. It is nevertheless helpful to assign the readings in this section. The excerpt from Robert Gordon's Enron article is especially good, since it situates counseling issues in context that have attracted widespread attention.

B. Family Practice

Family law is a field in which most lawyers agree that the counseling role is particularly important, because of the potential for human suffering, the possible conflicts between the needs of parents and children, and the difficulties that many clients experience in taking a long-term view of their best interests.

Many students will be drawn instinctively to the notion that lawyers in situations such as Problem 2(b) should represent the children's concerns as well as the parent's. For purposes of argument, it may be useful to invoke Richard Crouch's observation that the clients of "these self-righteous pontificators" are "not getting what they paid for." In his view, if you accept an adult's money intending to "really represent the child, there had better be an express declaration of who is getting your loyalty and your services, and an express waiver of the traditional attorney representation for fees received."[1] Under Crouch's analysis, another problem with the paternalistic role is that "what sometimes looks like the experienced lawyer's fatherly contribution of perspective can be nothing but presumption, bias, and professional arrogance. Deciding that the client will get what the client ought to want, rather than what the client wants, would certainly amount to fraud if the practice of law were the commercial enterprise that some people think it is."[2]

C. Tax Practice

Problems 3 and **4** reflect problems in business and individual tax counseling. In connection with Problem 3, Corneel's study of Boston tax practitioners was conducted when the prevailing ethical authority was ABA Opinion 314. It required a "reasonable basis" for any position chosen. A useful question for class exploration is whether the ABA's revised opinion 82-352 significantly alters the standard. The Report of the Special Task Force on Formal Opinion 85-352 suggests strongly that the answer is yes.

To illustrate difficulties in interpreting the "reasonable basis" and "realistic possibility of success" standards, professors can ask students to quantify their meanings. Each student should write on a piece of paper how likely (expressed in percentage terms) a position must be to prevail for it to satisfy these standards (e.g., 60%, 40%, 20%). The range of estimates, particularly for the reasonable basis test, can be illuminating.

Problem 4 brings out the tension between form and substance in compliance with legal rules. As the notes following the problem suggest, parallel dilemmas can arise in other forms of practice. Students may nevertheless feel that tax is different – that fudging on reportable income, as

---

[1] Richard Crouch, "When Responsibilities Overlap . . . How to Handle Conflicts of Interest," 9 *Fam. Advoc.* 4, 5 (Winter 1987).

[2] Id.

well as rearranging conduct and bookkeeping practices to minimize liability, is part of the American way of life. This is a perception that creates obvious problems for a system dependent on voluntary disclosure and compliance.

Exploration of such attitudes can also open the door to a discussion of problems with ethical relativism. For example, cynical students may be pressed about circumstances in which they would not accept "everyone does it" as a moral justification (such as overt racism in the South during the pre-Civil Rights era or acceptance of a child's explanation for cheating). As a very basic point, professors can remind students that counseling the client to pretend that she breeds poodles as a business is counseling her to commit fraud, in plain violation of Model Rule 1.2(d). What if she is asked under oath whether she raises her dogs for purposes of selling them? It is also useful to point out to students that tax cheats may raise the tax bill for everyone else. The federal government estimates an annual "tax gap" of about 14% of unpaid taxes, and that missing revenue may induce higher tax rates or fewer tax cuts, which harms honest compliers.

The material on tax shelters gives a sense of the competitive pressures that arise in tax practice as well as possible responses. Professors who are particularly interested in this area may want to show a CBS 60 minutes documentary from October 17, 2003, "Gimme Shelter," which discusses how those pressures have pushed most practitioners to lose "their moral bearing." Joseph Bankman, who is featured on the program, explains that the penalties are "an infinitesimal piece of the pie. If you compare the gross amount of taxes lost and the penalties levied, the ratio is 1000 to 1. . ." For a detailed discussion of tax penalties, arguing that they have been set too low, see Michael Doran, "Tax Penalties and Tax Compliance," forthcoming in 46 Harvard Journal on Legislation (2009).

The backdating issue in **Problem 6** is not, strictly speaking, a counseling problem; we have included it with the other tax problems because it generates good discussions. It is a hard case, not under code standards but under practical pressures. Students can speculate about what sort of pressure would be most compelling for them and how they might respond. For example, suppose the associate is struggling to pay his own student loans and his wife's graduate school tuition, while practicing in a small city with few firms in his specialty. Alternatively, assume that the managing partner's negligence had been attributable to her child's unexpected and critical illness. Discussion should also explore the psychological costs in practicing with attorneys willing to falsify documents to save their own skin. It is worth noting that those costs can be very hard to quantify but are often very real. Moreover, as Sissela Bok suggests in *Lying*, it is usually easy to tell a lie, but far more difficult to tell only one. If professors have not used the excerpts by Lewis and Schiltz in Chapter VII, they could be assigned in connection with this problem – Schiltz is particularly relevant, because he explicitly (and believably) mentions backdating documents as one of the steps on a young lawyer's descent into totally unethical practice.

In the case that inspired **Problem 6,** the associate circulated the memo, prevented the backdating, and, for the first time, received no annual bonus. He left the firm, had initial difficulties in finding a good alternative job, but ended up in a practice situation that was personally far more satisfying. Members of his firm had mixed reactions. Some admired the associate's courage and felt that his whistleblowing served a useful function. Others viewed his circulation of a memo (rather than some less public response) as cruel, unnecessarily self-righteous, and insensitive to the firm's potential liability.

Depending on the size of the class, it is often useful to discuss contexts in which students have faced similar problems. Emphasizing the value of peace of mind and a sense of personal integrity can be a way to broaden consideration of relevant concerns.

E. Government Lawyers

To raise the issue of how government lawyers should counsel clients, we have used one of the most controversial contexts in recent years: debates over the so-called "torture memos" issued by the Bush administration's Office of Legal Counsel (OLC). One in particular, the Bybee/Yoo memo, was widely criticized by most commentators for stretching the law in order to enable harsh treatment of detainees. Critics included several commentators who were generally sympathetic to the administration's policies. Of those cited in footnote 83 (p. 551), these include the Ramsey and Wedgwood/Woolsey articles. But the most noteworthy conservative critic was Jack Goldsmith, currently a professor at Harvard Law School. Goldsmith was a friend and ideological ally of John Yoo, who took over leadership of OLC soon after Yoo left. Goldsmith withdrew the Bybee/Yoo memo, and in his book *The Terror Presidency* (2007), describes it in harsh terms as a "golden shield" for lawbreakers. Id. at 162.

Goldsmith also writes that its treatment of the commander-in-chief's authority to override criminal prohibitions on torture "has no foundation in prior OLC opinions, or in judicial decisions, or in any other source of law." Id. at 149.

Rather than editorialize about the torture memos, we believe that the best way to teach them is simply by asking the students to examine them side-by-side with the statutes they are interpreting, and ask whether in students' view the statutes support the interpretation. But we also provide arguments about the memos through the words of other participants and commentators. Problem 7, combined with two sets of discussion questions (one on pages 553-54 and one on page 562) provide a straightforward way to organize class discussion.

Problem 7. (a) It seems clear that LTC Beaver's discussion of hiding operations from the ICRC is not legal advice, and may exceed the lawyer's role. Similarly, Mr. Fredman's advice about the "wet towel" technique (waterboarding), and about exploiting detainees' phobias, appears to be policy advice, not legal advice. We believe the most significant focus of discussion should be Mr. Fredman's analysis of the torture statute on pages 543-44. "...the language of the statutes is written vaguely" is clearly legal advice, and is a fair comment. "Severe mental and physical pain is prohibited" correctly states the statute (see 18 U.S.C. § 2340(1), reproduced on page 547). "The mental part is explained as poorly as the physical" is also a fair comment. But the next sentence is crucial: "Severe physical pain described as anything causing permanent physical damage to major organs or body parts" is nowhere to be found in the statute – but it IS found in the second paragraph of the Bybee/Yoo memo (p. 548) and the fourth paragraph (p. 549). This sentence clearly demonstrates that Fredman was familiar with the Bybee/Yoo memo. Fredman's explanation of what this standard implies is "It is basically subject to perception. If the detainee dies you're doing it wrong." It is crucial to the discussion to ask the students whether Fredman's explanation is or is not a fair inference from the Bybee/Yoo memo. (This is question 8, page 556.) This question will naturally guide them to answers to part (b). Finally, it is worth noting LTC Beaver's question about "imminent threat of death." Professors should point out that this phrase comes from the torture statute, 18 U.S.C. § 2340(2)(C), defining "severe mental pain or suffering." Thus, threats of imminent death are possible predicates for the crime of torture. Fredman does not point this out; instead, he merely states that it "should be handled on a case by case basis." If this is legal advice, it is bad legal advice. Part (c) allows the professor to discuss whether Fallon's outsider perspective is correct, and to discuss the problem of "groupthink" to those inside the discussion who did not notice what seems plain to Fallon.

Questions (pp. 554-56). Questions 2-6 are intended to guide a very concrete discussion of the possible legal infirmities of the torture memos.

Question 2. This asks whether a confidential legal opinion to a client should meet the same standard as an argument to a court (under MR 3.3(a)(2)). It is a hard question. No Model Rule requires divulging of adverse authority to a client with the same specificity as MR 3.3(a)(2); however, MR 2.1 requires lawyers to counsel clients with candor – and intuitively one might argue that legal advice given to a client should be *less* spun, not more spun, than legal argument to a court. The 1969 Code of Professional Responsibility states, "Where the bounds of law are uncertain, the action of a lawyer may depend on whether he is serving as advocate or advisor....[T]he two roles are essentially different....While serving as advocate, a lawyer should resolve in favor of his client doubts as to the bounds of the law. In serving a client as adviser, a lawyer in appropriate circumstances should give his professional opinion as to what the ultimate decisions of the courts would likely be as to the applicable law." On the other hand, the policy behind MR 3.3(a)(2) – making certain that judicial decisions are not made in inadvertent ignorance of all relevant authority – does not apply in the advisory context.

It is also debatable whether the authority that Professor Yoo omitted is directly adverse. The passage quoted from *Oakland Cannabis Buyers* leaves the existence of the necessity defense as an open question, and thus does not directly contradict the Bybee/Yoo discussion; however, it strongly hints that the Court might not recognize an extra-statutory necessity defense. As for the neglect of *Youngstown Sheet and Tube*, Professor Yoo writes the following in his memoir:

> We did not cite Justice Jackson's individual views in *Youngstown* because earlier OLC opinions, reaching across several administrations, had concluded that it had no application to the President's conduct of foreign affairs and national security. *Youngstown* reached the outcome it did because the Constitution clearly gives Congress, not the President, the exclusive power to make law concerning labor disputes...The Justice Department officials who launched the ethics investigation [of Professor Yoo] either ignored the department's long tradition in defending the President's commander-in-chief power or responded reflexively to political controversy....Claims about "ethics" always emerge as a

127

weapon, both on the left and the right, when the party in power cannot be budged on policy specifics.[1]

(It should be noted, however, that Professor Yoo's reading of *Youngstown* is not obviously correct. The Constitution also clearly gives Congress, not the President, the exclusive power to "define and punish crimes against the law of nations" such as torture; the torture statutes were written to implement the Torture Convention.)

Question 3. Most commentators reacted strongly against the "organ failure or death" standard of severe pain because it was drawn from a Medicare statute having nothing to do with torture – the reason given by OLC itself in the Levin memo, page 552, note 85.

Question 4. This and question 5 turn from the Bybee/Yoo memo to the less controversial Levin memo. In our opinion, there is nothing in the torture statute to justify the Levin memo's stipulation that physical suffering must be of "extended duration or persistence" to count as "severe" (p. 553). Just the opposite: the fact that the definition of *mental* suffering stipulates that it must be "prolonged" (18 U.S.C. §2340(2), p. 547), while there is no such stipulation about physical suffering, means under familiar canons of statutory construction that there is no duration requirement for physical suffering to count as severe. We believe that the best way to teach this question is simply to tell students to look at the statute on page 547, and then ask them where the Levin memo's duration requirement comes from.

Question 5. We believe that the best answer is that Levin memo might encourage harsh interrogation because waterboarding and stress positions are not as bad as the gruesome torture techniques listed on pp. 552-53. That is because an interrogator, looking to the memo for guidance, would naturally conclude that less atrocious interrogation methods are not prohibited.

Question 6. The Levin memo does not withdraw the Bybee/Yoo analysis

---

[1] John C. Yoo, *War By Other Means: An Insider's Account of the War on Terror* 184-85 (2006).

of presidential power (see p. 552); and indeed, a similar analysis appears in an OLC opinion of September 25, 2001 that has never been withdrawn. (It is available on the OLC website.) It does appear, however, that the Levin memo withdraws the discussion of self-defense and necessity. (P. 552: "This memorandum supersedes the August 2002 Memorandum in its entirety.")

The questions on page 562 are meant to stimulate broader discussion of policy.

CHAPTER X: CONFLICTS OF INTEREST

Our treatment of conflicts of interest includes the standard topics and typologies – concurrent representation of conflicting interests, former-client conflicts, vicarious disqualification, the former government lawyer, etc. It also focuses primary attention on those aspects of conflicts that expose underlying normative issues. Thus, we devote more attention than is typical to criminal defense, because this area highlights the elusive matter of when multiple interests clash and when they harmonize. Similarly, we include Thomas Shaffer's provocative argument that conflicts rules are based on a faulty moral premise of radical individualism, because this charge raises central ethical concerns. We also include substantial material on conflicts in class actions, because these have always been issues of great public significance. Conflict of interest is often treated as a largely doctrinal and technical part of the legal ethics course, with less "human interest" than other pieces of the course. We disagree, and the present chapter aims throughout to raise issues that are engaging on the human as well as the doctrinal level.

Doing It Quickly

A bare-bones version of Chapter X could include the following: the introduction, excluding *U.S. v. Bronston*; *Cuyler v. Sullivan* and the accompanying questions, Problem 1 together with the Shaffer excerpt and accompanying notes, and *Westinghouse v. Kerr-McGee* (on simultaneous representation); all of Section D (on former-client conflicts); all of Section E (on imputed disqualification); and at least some review of Model Rules 1.8 (miscellaneous conflicts of interest, perhaps Problems 11 and/or 12 and/or the "sexy" Problem 13), 1.11 (former government lawyers, perhaps Problem 6 and 3.7 (the advocate-witness rule). This could take four classroom hours – one each for concurrent conflicts, former-client conflicts, imputed disqualification, and the other conflicts of interest. However, treating conflicts so briefly omits subjects that are fun to discuss, important, or both – the stonewall defense, positional conflicts of interest, and conflicts in class actions. Professors who want to include this material may wish to drop the criminal defense section or expand the discussion to six class hours.

A. Introduction

The introduction focuses on the principal practical difference between conflicts rules and other ethical rules: the availability of disqualification remedies, and the possibility for tactical use and abuse of conflicts rules.

United States v. Bronston

Bronston, like the *Cueto* case in Chapter IV, serves to remind students that breaches of legal ethics can land a lawyer in jail. Here, the biggest difficulty lies in determining exactly what it was that justified convicting Bronston of mail fraud. The court denies that its holding means that any disloyal or unethical act by a lawyer (accompanied by a mailing) is a sufficient basis for criminal liability. However, the court admits that a hypothetical situation could be constructed in which its theory of the case yields this result even though no damage to the disloyal lawyer's client resulted. The court then suggests that in the case at bar, the aggrieved client actually lost money. This argument plainly implies that the court does *not* think that disloyalty in and of itself is fraudulent; only disloyalty accompanied by harm is fraudulent. That theory might make sense if it wasn't for another part of the court's argument. The court reasons that the element establishing fraud was Bronston's nondisclosure, not his disloyalty; but it was only the disloyalty that injured the client. What is the theory of the case? Teachers can press Question 2 (p. 570) to bring home how elusive the court's theory is. We can conclude from *Bronston* that when a lawyer, utilizing the mails, (a) is disloyal to a client, and (b) fails to disclose the disloyalty, and (c) harms the client, the lawyer has committed mail fraud. But the court never tells us which of these three elements is essential.

Question 3 (p. 570) raises an important issue. Although it did not choose to do so, the prosecution in *Bronston* could have used a very broad theory to establish mail fraud. In a long line of cases, federal courts have upheld mail fraud convictions of dishonest employees who breached a fiduciary obligation to their employer, on the ground that the employee has defrauded the employer of an "intangible right of honest services," whether or not the employer suffered any tangible harm.[2] A typical "intangible right of honest services" case involves

---

[2] See, e.g., United States v. George, 477 F.2d 508 (7th Cir.), cert. denied, 414 U.S. 827 (1973).

an employee, or sometimes a public official, who awards contracts to contractors paying him kickbacks. Sometimes it cannot be shown that the employer was harmed, because the contractor gives good service at a fair price. Nevertheless, it seems that such corruption is fraudulent, and the fraud that courts traditionally identified was depriving the employer of the intangible right of honest services. However, after *McNally v. United States*, 483 U.S. 350 (1987) rejected this theory, Congress responded by enacting 18 U.S.C. § 1346, quoted in footnote 12 (p. 570), which explicitly states that mail and wire frauds include any "scheme or artifice to deprive another of the intangible right of honest services."

Caveat advocatus! Under section 1346, any lawyer who betrays a client, using the mails or the wires (or Fed Ex), is guilty of mail or wire fraud. This follows whether or not the client is harmed by the lawyer's betrayal. In other words, § 1346 makes disloyalty accompanied by a mailing a federal offense. It remains to be seen how often and under what circumstances prosecutors will pursue lawyers.

B. Conflicts of Interest in Criminal Defense

This section involves two major clusters of issues. The first concerns the constitutional questions surrounding multiple representation of criminal defendants, while the second concerns the tactical and moral issues involved in using multiple representation to "stonewall" an investigation, that is, to choreograph a defense based on information control.

The first subsection is organized around *Cuyler v. Sullivan*. *Cuyler* holds that a trial judge's failure to investigate and remedy possible conflicts in multiple representation of criminal defendants does not in itself violate a defendant's sixth amendment right: it does so only if the multiple representation generates an actual conflict of interest adversely affecting representation. Questions 1, 2, and 3 following *Cuyler* merit especially careful classroom discussion. Question 1 distinguishes the different standards debated in the opinion, and it helps if the teacher walks through these in some detail. Particularly important is the point that Justice Marshall quotes from *Holloway v. Arkansas*: "[T]o assess the impact of a conflict of interests on the attorney's options, tactics, and decisions in plea negotiations would be virtually impossible." Question 2 highlights the fact that when co-defendants have adverse interests, separate representation will not necessarily benefit them. True, their own lawyers will no longer compromise their defense, but the zealous advocacy of a codefendant's lawyer may be even more devastating.

Yet whenever we ask whether a lawyer facing an actual conflict offers impaired representation, we must also ask, "compared with what?" The conflicts described in Question 3 will be cured by separate representation, but this may make little difference in outcome for the clients. Consider, for example, Question 3(c), concerning the difficulty a single lawyer faces in advising multiple defendants whether or not to testify. As Geer notes, "If...only one of an attorney's two clients takes the witness stand, the lawyer must contend with the inevitable question in the minds of the jurors as to why the other defendant refused to testify." Surely the same question would occur to the jurors if the two defendants were represented separately, so curing the conflict may do nothing to help prevent the adverse inferences.

Question 4, p. 577.

In *Wheat*, the likelihood that Gomez-Barajas's plea-bargain will be turned down, thereby landing Iredale in a conflict of interest, is very slight. The likelihood that Bravo will testify, on the other hand, is high (because the prosecution has added him to the witness list). But, as Justice Marshall indicated in his dissent, the conflict would not be particularly severe, because Wheat's testimony had little bearing on Bravo's case – indeed, Wheat claimed never to have met Bravo. The likely damage of a conflict of interest can be minimal either because its probability is low, or because its outcome is not severe.

Mickens v. Taylor is included in part because of its remarkable facts and holding – the Supreme Court finds no constitutional violation when a capital defendant's lawyer had represented the murder victim at the time of the murder. (Note that the facts of the case are summarized on page 578, just before the case itself.) But we also include the decision because Justice Scalia's opinion includes an extremely clear summary of the Court's conflicts doctrine, which will prove very useful for students.

The stonewalling material includes a thought-provoking excerpt from Kenneth Mann's investigation of the white-collar bar, followed on pp. 587-88 by an analysis based on the game-theory problem of the Prisoner's Dilemma. In applying the Prisoner's Dilemma analysis to the stonewalling problem, it is useful to stress the lawyer's role in coordinating the defendants' choices. The lawyer is able to say to each client "If you decide to accept the prosecutor's offer, I will have to advise your co-defendant to do the same; but if you decide to reject the prosecutor's offer, I will advise your co-defendant to do so as well." By counseling the clients in this way, the defense lawyer makes it very likely that each will do whatever the other does. If the second client insists on dealing with the prosecutor, and instructs the lawyer to keep this decision confidential, the lawyer must reply that, even with confidentiality, professional duty requires advising the co-defendant to deal with the prosecutor. This is how the defense lawyer can make it rational for co-defendants to stonewall even in a Prisoner's Dilemma.

In such a case, an odd, almost paradoxical result follows. Even though the defendants' interests would conflict if they were represented separately – each of their attorneys should advise them to deal, because of the usual Prisoner's Dilemma -- their interests don't conflict when they are represented by a single lawyer.

The discussion then switches from the perspective of the defense to the perspective of law-enforcement. Some courts have tried to use the putative conflict of interest to disqualify defense counsel not to protect clients but to prevent stonewalling. *Pirillo v. Takiff* is an example of such a case. Professors might suggest that this represents an abuse of the conflict-of-interest rules, and that if courts intend to end multiple representation as a way of attacking stonewalling, they should do so directly by enacting rules forbidding multiple representation, either per se or in stonewalling contexts. Professors may then ask students whether such a rule would violate either the due-process or right-to-counsel provisions of the Constitution.

C. Concurrent Representation of Conflicting Interests in Civil Matters

Thomas Shaffer's essay pursues the question of whether individual interests are the be-all and end-all of legal ethics. We have found that Shaffer's Case of the Unwanted Will, together with his unabashed anti-individualism, make the essay quite rewarding to teach.

Typically, students resist Shaffer's strongly interventionist approach to

134

the problem, summarized in the final sentence of the excerpt: they regard his suggestion that the lawyer try to force the issue of determining "whether this family is equal to the truth of what it is" as wholly inappropriate. Often, students respond along the lines of "I'm a lawyer, not a therapist!" Interestingly, however, an experienced estates-and-trusts practitioner to whom we showed the problem reported that she and many of her colleagues would deal with the situation precisely as Shaffer suggests. She added that estate planning is a legal specialty in which sensitive counseling about delicate emotional issues is an important and frequently exercised skill. She added that lawyers who aren't good at dealing with issues that are fraught with emotion for clients should not become estate planners. Death is a touchy subject.

Many students argue that a lawyer should not draft both spouse's wills (a suggestion frequently at odds with actual practice). Others believe that John and Mary's lawyer must withdraw the moment the conflict surfaces. A third common response is that if Mary consents to sign the will, even though she is unhappy with it, that should be the end of the matter: the lawyer should proceed without further interruption. To this argument, it is helpful to stress the seriousness of the matter at issue. It is not sheer sentimentality that leads the lawyer to insist that the client's last will and testament really represent her will. It is also useful to point out that if Mary had firmly determined to go along with John despite her wishes, she didn't have to tell the lawyer that the will was not to her liking. Under the circumstances, the lawyer should interpret Mary's answer as an ambivalent request for help.

Some students also attempt to analyze the problem by reference to MR 1.13 (on organizational clients), as though the best way to understand a family is by pretending that it is a corporation. One reply is that this approach simply confirms Shaffer's point -- that the family, as basic an institution as any in social life, becomes unintelligible when viewed through the individualistic lens of the ethics rules.

Some students object to the idea that Mary's wishes should be subordinated to John's, and view that prospect as a reflection and reinforcement of gender inequality. This is an important objection, but the teacher should take care to explain that Shaffer agrees with it. His argument that the interests of the family take precedence over those of individuals may sound superficially like the proposal that Mary should subordinate her wishes in the interest of family harmony. But in fact that is just the opposite of Shaffer's proposal. He insists that Mary's view of who belongs to the family *cannot* be dismissed or ignored: that is why the lawyer should encourage her to raise the issue with John.

Finally, students often reply that Shaffer has an unrealistic belief in family harmony. This view, however, underestimates his position. Shaffer's point in picking the opening quotation from Ann Tyler is that families are *not* harmonious – they are *cracked* magnifying glasses – but they are the only lens that permits us to make sense of what family members do. That is not to deny the problems with Shaffer's approach. The discussion questions in the text are intended to explore the limitations of his analysis.

The section then shifts gears, and reexamines simultaneous representation issues in a variety of business contexts.

Problem 2 is a familiar one to those who followed the very acrimonious debate over standards for insurance defense lawyers in the *Restatement*. We summarize the principal arguments on the two sides of the debate and explain what is at stake, namely whether the insurer or the insured controls controversial aspects of the defense. Proponents of the traditional one-client view won the battle over the *Restatement*, but Problem 2 – based on the often-cited *Montanez v. Irizarry-Rodriguez* case cited in note 44, p. 603 – presents a scenario that is a kind of poster child for the two-client view. The client defendant wishes to throw the case so that the plaintiff – his wife – collects the maximum amount of insurance money. On the one-client view, the lawyer must help the client lose his case. In the actual *Montanez* case, the lawyer asked the court to treat his client as a hostile witness, savagely cross-examined him to show that he had committed perjury, and "won" his case for him (thereby doing the opposite of what he wanted). On appeal the New Jersey court found the attorney's behavior outrageous and reversed and remanded.

Westinghouse v. Kerr-McGee, the major case in this section, raises two major doctrinal issues: the use of Chinese wall screening techniques in order to avoid law firm disqualification; and the applicability of conflicts rules to entities that are not actually clients. *Westinghouse* is the primary authority for the rejection of screening in simultaneous representation contexts. The discussion questions focus on whether it is realistic to regard a very large law firm as a conductor of information rather than an insulator. On the one hand, it is tempting to agree with the *Westinghouse* court that it would be objectionable to employ different ethical standards for large and small law firms; on the other hand, the fiction of shared confidences is less plausible in the large firm context.

The second issue arises when a firm represents a client against an adversary organization that either includes, or is part of, another of the firm's clients. *Westinghouse* insists that the test of adverse interests is functional, not nominal: though Kirkland, Ellis represented API, not its member companies, it was in fact acting as counsel to the member companies, who it was simultaneously suing on behalf of Westinghouse. This edition of *Legal Ethics* explores the practical problems this holding creates for large law firms trying to identify conflicts when they must check not only the nominal client, but its corporate subsidiaries and the corporate families to which it belongs as well.

Problem 3 (p. 609) raises various examples of *positional* conflicts of interest. Positional conflicts are at the cutting edge of current interest, and many teachers will find the Spaulding article cited in note 56, and John S. Dzienkowski, "Positional Conflicts of Interest," 71 Tex. L. Rev. 457 (1993) useful in class preparation.

a) It is wholly proper for the lawyer to belong to an environmentalist organization, but Model Rule 6.3(a) makes it clear that the lawyer cannot litigate against the firm's client. The firm's memorandum is wrong, and perhaps disingenuous, in asserting a conflicts problem. This is a pure business conflict: the firm does not want to antagonize its wealthy client.

b) Perhaps the most interesting question arising from part (b) concerns the imputed conflict of interest. Although the two lawyers belong to the same firm, the pro bono organizations they wish to work for have no connection with each other, and any conflict of interest arising under Model Rule 1.7 would concern the pro bono organizations rather than the law firm and its clients. Should the interests of the pro bono organizations be imputed to each other via Barnes & Chippe? If not, the conflict of interest is a pseudo-conflict.

It could be argued that the partner who wants the firm to establish a committee to screen firm lawyers' pro bono cases is interfering improperly with matters that really are not the firm's business. Rule 6.1 states that a lawyer should provide pro bono assistance, and Rules 6.3 and 6.4 state that, so long as

137

the lawyer is not violating Rule 1.7 or improperly curtailing representation of the pro bono client on behalf of another client, the representation is proper. Rule 5.1(a) holds law firm partners responsible for making "reasonable efforts to ensure that the firm has in effect measures giving reasonable assurance that all lawyers in the firm conform to the Rules of Professional Conduct" – and the partner in this problem seems to making efforts to undercut pro bono activities that are commended in Rule 6.1 and in conformity with 6.3 and 6.4. On the other hand, if the firm is subsidizing pro bono work by providing secretarial and other assistance, or by giving billable hour credit, then it could be argued that the members should have some say in the causes that they are supporting. Firm oversight can also be a way of channeling scarce resources to the most needy causes rather than to matters that will benefit the lawyers' own friends, family, or favorite charities.

c) Here comment [24] to Model Rule 1.7 provides the basis for discussion. Positional conflicts in litigation pose two distinct issues. First, lawyers or law firms risk undercutting their credibility by arguing opposite positions before the same court, at either the trial or appellate level. Lawyers report that this risk is slight before a tribunal as sophisticated as the Delaware Chancery Court, which confronts the same law firms arguing both sides of complex corporate issues on a regular basis. Matters may be quite different if a court confronts such side-switching rarely. Second, when the issue is argued before an appellate court, a favorable decision in one case may set a precedent precluding favorable resolution of the other client's case. In short, the issues are *credibility* and *preclusion*.

d) This situation does not represent a true conflict under Rule 1.7, as comment [6] to the rule makes clear ("simultaneous representation in unrelated matters of clients whose interests are only economically adverse, such as representation of competing economic enterprises in unrelated litigation, does not ordinarily constitute a conflict of interest and thus may not require consent of the respective clients."). However, it may be an important practical conflict, particularly if Ecoclean represents a sizable portion of the firm's billings.

A noteworthy example of a business conflict of interest was reported in the *New York Times*. The well-known law firm of Weil, Gotschal & Manges withdrew from its pro bono representation of New York City in lawsuits against gun manufacturers after Smith & Wesson (a gun manufacturer) persuaded a corporate client of the firm to pressure it to withdraw.[3]

D. Conflicts Involving Former Clients

Problem 4 is meant to clarify the "substantially related" standard of Model Rule 1.9, which derives from *T.C. Theatre v. Warner Bros.* On our analysis, the answers to the questions are as follows:

a) On the *Gulf Oil* test, the matters are substantially related if it is reasonable to assume that the lawyer has received confidential information from the former client that would be relevant to the present case; and, on the test given in Comment [3] to Rule 1.9, the matters are substantially related if in addition the confidential information would advance the interests of Insatiable Industries. It is reasonable to infer that when your firm negotiated the labor contract with the union, it received a great deal of confidential information about the firm's profitability and business prospects, because this is information essential to contract negotiations. Unions predicate their demands on their assessment of how well the company is doing, and management must be prepared to argue specifics. Thus, here the matters are substantially related on either test, and the firm cannot represent Insatiable Industries.

b) The problem specifies that in preparing the cert petition "no lawyer in your firm acquired confidential information from Tidbit," and this stipulation makes the problem relatively easy. Under Rule 1.9(b), the representation is permissible, whether or not the matters are substantially related. In any event, the two matters probably aren't substantially related. On the *Gulf Oil* test, the matters are substantially related only if it is reasonable to suppose that the firm received client confidences from Tidbit that would be useful in its representation of Insatiable; and there is no reason to suppose it on these facts, because the cert petition is based entirely on the record and on strictly legal issues.

---

[3] William Glaberson, "New York Loses Major Legal Ally In Suit Over Guns," *N.Y. Times*, April 17, 2004, at A1

However, as noted in D.C. Bar Ethics Opinion 343, "even in litigation before the Supreme Court on what appears to be a purely legal issue, confidential factual information may turn out to be useful to a lawyer." The lawyer may, for example, serve as lead coordinator of amicus briefs, a task for which factual information may be necessary. The opinion continues: "We are mindful of the Court of Appeals' admonition in *In re Sofaer*, that even if a lawyer sincerely believes that his or her representation 'could be insulated, factually and ethically,' from the earlier representation, the belief might be mistaken. In that case, '[t]he "substantially related" test by its terms, ... is meant to induce a ... lawyer considering a representation to err well on the side of caution.' 728 A.2d at 628."

c) The answer to this question is given in the text on pages 615-16. Under standard doctrine, as summarized in the Restatement, § 132, cmt. *b*, a lawyer may not seek to discredit work he or she has done for a former client. Thus, it is impermissible for the firm to represent Insatiable Industries, since that requires challenging the poison pill bylaws that it had drafted.

d) The problem here is whether Tidbit is a former or current client. The situation is essentially one described by Professor Wolfram in "Former-Client Conflicts," 10 *Georgetown Journal of Legal Ethics* 677, 703 (1997): "A client, considering whether to acquire a business, first comes to a lawyer for advice about legal implications of the purchase, receives the advice, and leaves saying that the client will get back to the lawyer if and when the client decides to proceed. The lawyer smiles and gives an ambiguous farewell. If the lawyer hears nothing further from the client for several months, is the representation over? When, precisely, did it end? Prudent lawyers may send a termination letter." The leading case *IBM v. Levin*, 579 F.2d 271 (3d Cir. 1978), held that a year of inactivity in a long-standing attorney-client relationship was not enough to turn a current client into a former client. But in the present problem, the attorney-client relationship was neither intensive nor extensive, and the "reasonable client" probably should not expect loyalty from counsel under such casual circumstances. Thus, the representation is very likely permissible.

e) Dropping the trademark case to represent Tidbit's adversary violates the "hot potato" rule. But there is some debate over how well-founded the hot potato rule is in the black letter of the Model Rules. Model Rule 1.16(b)(1), on permissive withdrawal, appears to countenance withdrawing from a case for any reason or no reason at all, provided that doing so does not harm the client. That includes withdrawing in order to represent a different client, and even if the new client is attacking the dropped client in an unrelated matter.[4] Since the problem stipulates that withdrawing from the current representation of Tidbit Technologies would not injure Tidbit in any tangible way, Rule 1.16(b) permits the withdrawal. However, the *Restatement* disagrees and endorses the hot potato rule, arguing that "[a] premature withdrawal violates the lawyer's obligation of loyalty to the existing client and can constitute a breach of the client-lawyer contract of employment." Restatement, § 132, cmt. *c.* As Hazard and Hodes note, regardless of its basis in the rules, the hot potato rule represents the law in some jurisdictions.

f) Intuitively, it seems that the bad faith of the client in "planting" the trademark case invites a similar response from the law firm, but the hot potato rule (if it *is* a rule! – see the preceding paragraph) does not contain an exception for canny, manipulative clients. The trademark case may have been planted, and it may be relatively small – but it is a genuine piece of legal business, which the firm accepted with eyes wide open.

g) In answering this question, see the material on advance waivers on pp. 622-624. Admittedly, the waiver covers the facts of this case, because the trademark case is very likely not substantially related to the hostile takeover (although there may be a remote possibility that the trademark is central to Tidbit's business prospects). However, ABA Formal Opinion 93-372 (1993) cautions that such blanket advance waivers are not per se valid, and must be revisited when a potential conflict actually arises. In the present case, where the "directly adverse" representation amounts to a mortal threat to Tidbit Technology's

---

[4] See Geoffrey C. Hazard, Jr. & W. William Hodes, 1 *The Law of Lawyering* (3rd ed. 2001), §20.10.

corporate existence, it is inconceivable that the representation would be permitted under Model Rule 1.7.

***

Westinghouse v. Gulf Oil includes a clear three-step articulation of the most common test of whether a former and current representation are substantially related. That test understands matters to be substantially related if they involve a significant risk of using the former client's confidences against that client's interests. It is very much in the spirit of Judge Weinfeld's original *T.C. Theatre* opinion, as well as in Comment [3] to Model Rule 1.9.

E. Imputed Disqualification

Problem 5 is meant to provide a straightforward exercise in applying Model Rules 1.9 and 1.10. We have found that many students have a difficult time with these rules, and that an exercise such as this is more appropriate than a more analytical problem. The answers are as follows:

1. a) No to Senior Partner, unless Client One consents in writing. Model Rule 1.9(a). No to any lawyer in Baker & Baker. Model Rule 1.10(a). No to any lawyer in Baker & Baker even if Senior Partner is screened, since Model Rule 1.10(a) makes no provision for screening. However, as note 65 points out, screening cures imputed disqualification under certain circumstances in several states. Furthermore, §124(2) of the *Restatement* permits other Baker & Baker lawyers to undertake the representation provided that

"there is no substantial risk that confidential information of the former client will be used with material adverse effect on the former client because:

(a) any confidential client information communicated to the personally prohibited lawyer is unlikely to be significant in the subsequent matter;

(b) the personally prohibited lawyer is subject to screening measures adequate to eliminate participation by that lawyer in the representation; and

(c) timely and adequate notice of the screening has been provided to all affected clients."

b) No to Junior Partner, unless Client One consents. Model Rule 1.9(b). No to any lawyer in Baker & Baker, with or without screening. Model Rule 1.10(a).

c) Yes to Associate. Model Rule 1.9(b)(2). Yes to any lawyer in Baker & Baker. Model Rule 1.10(a), with or without screening.
2. No.

3. a) Yes. Model Rule 1.10(b).

b) Yes. So long as Adams & Adams retains the case file, lawyers remaining in the firm "have" information protected by Rules 1.6 and 1.9(c), which is the requirement for imputed disqualification under 1.10(b)(2). However, if Adams & Adams returns the case file to Client One unread, and is able to prove this to the satisfaction of a court -- typically through affidavits -- then the firm will be able to avoid disqualification.

The main case in this section is the familiar *Silver Chrysler Plymouth* decision. It concerns what might be called the Case of the Ambulatory Associate: a large-firm associate who worked only on the fringes of a case, without acquiring client confidences, and then switched jobs. To disqualify him, and his entire new firm, from representation on matters adverse to his former client would drastically and needlessly limit career mobility for young lawyers. The only complexity in the case lies in explaining why Schreiber should not be irrebuttably presumed to have acquired Chrysler's confidences, as *T.C. Theatre* requires. *Silver Chrysler* solves the problem by holding that Schreiber did not actually "represent" the former client. Permitting Schreiber to be screened would be an alternative approach, rejected by Model Rule 1.10 but accepted in §124(2) of the *Restatement*.

As the casebook went to press, the ABA at its August 2008 meeting considered a proposal by the ABA Ethics Committee to amend Model Rule 1.10 to allow screening of a lawyer who joins a firm and would be personally disqualified from representing one of the firm's clients. In effect, the proposal revives the lateral screening modification recommended by the Ethics 2000 Commission and rejected by the House of Delegates in 2001. Lawrence Fox, who led the fight in 2001, denounced the current proposal as a "terrible tragic idea" that puts "lawyer convenience way ahead of client loyalty."[5] The ABA has deferred decision on the amendment.

---

[5] Joan C. Rodgers, "ABA to consider Amending Model Rules to Let Firms Use Screening for Lateral Hires," 24 ABA/BNA Laywer Manual Prof Conduct 324 (June 25, 2008) (quoting Fox).

F. The Former Government Lawyer

Problem 6 is governed by Model Rule 1.11(a) and 3.5(b) and the "forever rule" in 18 U.S.C.A. §207(a)(1). The threshold question in all of these is whether the current antitrust litigation is the same "matter" as the preparation of the position paper for the Antitrust Division. Assume that the answer is yes, because the attorney had access to deliberations and information in the Antitrust Division that will be useful in the litigation. Under both the Model Rules and the Code (as interpreted in *Armstrong v. McAlpin*, following ABA Formal Opinion 342), the answer to Question 1 is that the lawyer may participate in the litigation only provided that the Antitrust Division consents; but even without the Division's consent other lawyers in the firm may participate in the litigation provided that the personally-disqualified lawyer is screened. However, §207(a)(1) forbids the lawyer from participating personally in the litigation. Model Rule 3.5(b) prohibits the lawyer from contacting officials in the Antitrust Division unless applicable law permits it. The same statute, §207(a)(1), forbids such contact if it is undertaken "with the intent to influence." Thus, whether the lawyer may contact friends in the Antitrust Division will turn on whether the aim of the conversation is influence or merely inquiry. Model Rule 3.9 requires the lawyer to disclose to officials in the Division that he or she is representing an adversary in the matter.

Our principal case in this section is the familiar *Armstrong v. McAlpin* decision. On the surface, the issue it addresses is fairly clear. Strict imputed disqualification for firms employing former government lawyers would reduce opportunities for firms to curry favor by playing on agency lawyers' hopes for future employment. On the other hand, closing the revolving door in this way would dissuade ambitious attorneys from entering public service. The costs would be born by both government and the private sector, which would be unable to draw on the expertise of former insiders. Balancing these competing considerations, the *Armstrong* court decided to leave the revolving door ajar. It is worth exploring whether an unstated assumption is that former government lawyers are more readily trusted to comply with screening procedures than other lawyers. Alternatively, is the assumption that the risks of abuse are the same but that costs of minimizing those risks are greater for government lawyers?

Underlying both sides of the debate, however, is the unquestioned premise that talented individuals will enter government service only if they believe that it will enhance future employment opportunities. Perhaps this is true; if so, however, it indicates something of a chasm between contemporary mores and the civic ideals of the founding era. As Garry Wills argues in *Explaining America*, the political theory of the Federalist Papers assumed that without a modicum of public-regarding civic virtue, the new-fledged republic could not survive. Students may usefully explore whether the premise of self-interest underlying *Armstrong* is inconsistent with this assumption. We believe that the revolving door issue can make a useful springboard for a broader discussion of whether there is anything ethically distinctive about government law practice – whether, that is, the authors of the Federalist were right in supposing that government employees would exhibit special concern for the public interest.

The section closes by asking whether a lawyer representing "the public" has an independent obligation to assess its interests, or whether the government lawyer must simply follow the instructions of superiors who may be politically motivated – this, we take it, is another way of getting at the issue of whether government service presupposes some special concern for the public good.

G . Conflicts of Interest in Class Actions

Issues concerning class actions have become increasingly prominent since the tobacco and asbestos litigation and the Supreme Court's *Amchem* and *Fiberboard* decisions, and problems involving conflicts of interest, attorneys' fees, and confidential settlements continue to attract substantial controversy.

Problem 7 is a structural reform case modeled on the Pennhurst litigation. The issues it raises are discussed in the Rhode excerpt, and also in Derrick Bell's famous article "Serving Two Masters," which argues that NAACP lawyers pursuing school desegregation on behalf of African-American communities who did not necessarily want it faced a debilitating conflict of interest. The conflict Bell described is a longstanding one. Indeed, it was precisely this issue that led W.E.B. DuBois to resign from the NAACP, which he had helped found. DuBois believed that school improvement held out some promise of making African-American life better, unlike the pursuit of school desegregation, which DuBois believed to be a hopeless ideal.

Questions, pp. 650-51

1. In view of the deep rift within the Pennhurst class between those parents and guardians who desired community placements and those who opposed such placements, it is debatable whether a single lawyer can represent the class adequately. The strongest argument for an affirmative answer is that the interests of the class, which in effect includes future residents of Pennhurst, may not be identical with the majority of the present class. Indeed, it is not obvious that the guardians and next friends of current residents represent those residents' interests with complete disinterest. As David Luban has written, "If the class action has significant implications for future generations, a nose count of the living may well overlook the majority of noses."[6]

2. Under Model Rule 1.2(c), "a lawyer may limit the scope of the representation if the limitation is reasonable under the circumstances

---

[6] David Luban, *Lawyers and Justice: An Ethical Study* 347 (1988).

and the client gives informed consent." But it is far from obvious that the consent of named plaintiffs in a class action should bind all the unnamed class members. In our view, the problem that client consent was supposed to solve – adequacy of representation of disparate class interests by class lawyers – is really no different from the problem that this consent creates: the adequacy of representation of disparate class interests by named plaintiffs, many of whom may have been recruited to the task by the lawyers. And consenting to representation "consistent with the goals of the Disability Rights Defense Fund" is particularly suspicious, because here it seems that the named plaintiffs are ceding their own judgment to the lawyers. Bringing suit on behalf of a single individual or an organization rather than a class would solve the Rule 23 problems, but not the substantive moral dilemma: should the lawyers be taking positions on behalf of individuals who actively oppose those positions?

3. The final question, about the differences between representing a discrete client group and a large, amorphous class, lends itself to an obvious answer: the more amorphous the class, the less the practical possibility of consulting with representative members and the greater the responsibility assumed by the lawyers. In Pennhurst, the lawyers could more readily be bound by a majority vote of the class members than in large school desegregation cases.[7] However, both contexts present questions about whether parents of current plaintiffs are well positioned to speak for the long term interests of all those who will be affected by the decree.

Fiandaca v. Cunningham

This case is quite straightforward to teach. The major question raised by the court's decision is whether it provides a weapon to class action defendants seeking to delay or derail a suit. A settlement that helps one client at the expense of the other will present a conflict of interest that may require disqualification. In *Fiandaca*, the issue is whether the State of New Hampshire, which had been fighting for years to delay upgrading the facilities for female inmates, has offered the

---

[7] See id., at 347-54.

Laconia State School merely to disqualify New Hampshire Legal Assistance at the last minute. The court says no, because "There is simply no evidence to support plaintiffs' suggestion that the state 'created' the conflict by intentionally offering plaintiffs a building at LSS in an effort 'to dodge the bullet again'. . . ."

Question 2 (p. 663) asks what the evidence is for and against this analysis of the state's motivation. As we see it, the evidence that the state's motivation really was just tactical is as follows. First, the timing is suspicious; the state's attorneys did not offer the LSS facility until two weeks before trial, when they could have done so much earlier. Waiting until the last minute maximizes the delay if the trial court grants the motion to disqualify. And if the trial court refuses to grant the motion to disqualify because of its last-minute character, this creates an appealable issue and further delays. Second, after the hearing the parties negotiated a settlement that would in effect have called the state's bluff, and accepted the offer of LSS -- and NHLA withdrew as counsel. But the state refused to sign the settlement, suggesting that it made its offer in bad faith.

There is also evidence that the state's offer was not merely tactical: First, the state had made an earlier proposal, which the plaintiffs had rejected. Second, in the early stages of the litigation, "NHLA lawyers and their trial expert . . . twice toured and examined potential facilities . . . including buildings at the Laconia State School. . . ." So the LSS possibility was on the table, and known to plaintiffs' counsel, well in advance of the state's pre-trial offer. Professors can draw their own conclusions or leave it to students to decide.

Question 3 asks whether NHLA's lawyers should have realized at the time that they toured LSS that they might have a potential conflict of interest. If so, should they have tried to find alternative counsel? The *Garrity* litigation was already well underway. It had been filed in 1979, and Judge Devine's ruling dated from 1981. *Garrity v. Gallen*, 522 F.Supp. 171 (Dist. N.H. 1981). However, the attorneys may well have reasoned that the state would not or could not offer a facility at LSS precisely because it would violate Judge Devine's remedial order. NHLA argued that it had no conflict of interest because Judge Loughlin indicated that he would not approve a settlement that undercut the

Garrity order by harming members of the *Garrity* class in any way. It is somewhat baffling why the First Circuit did not accept this argument. We don't know why NHLA had taken over the case; perhaps Bertram Astles, the inmates's first lawyer, was unable to continue. NHLA lawyers may have believed that, as the only legal aid organization in the state, they had to take the risk that no conflict of interest would materialize, because otherwise one or the other plaintiff class would have no counsel.

2. Mass Torts; Problem 8

Although the mass torts material is complex, we believe that it is both important and rewarding. It raises some of the most important ethical issues on today's legal landscape. The discussion should center around Problem 8.

Problem 8 is closely modeled on the consolidated asbestos settlement negotiated and approved in *Georgine v. Amchem, Inc.*, later rejected by the Third Circuit Court of Appeals and then by the Supreme Court in *Amchem v. Windsor*. The principal difference between the facts in Problem 8 and the asbestos settlement appears in the final paragraph of the problem, just before the questions: the UC-55 complaint will seek to certify a number of subclasses rather than a single class. The reason for this difference is straightforward: *Amchem* disapproved the asbestos settlement because of the disparity among the interests of the different subgroups within the class. Hence, the UC-55 settlement could not treat all present and future UC-55 victims as members of a single class.

Notice also the fee arithmetic in this problem. The problem stipulates that class members will receive payouts ranging from $7,500 to $75,000, ten to twenty percent lower than the average payouts for corresponding injuries litigated individually. However, plaintiffs bringing their cases individually pay higher attorneys' fees – a typical contingency fee would be 33% - 40%. Under the settlement, attorneys' fees are capped at 25%, so the client will net 75% of the settlement payout. If the client litigates individually, and receives an award ten percent higher than the settlement payout, he or she will net 73% of the settlement payout if the attorney's fee is a 33% contingency fee, but only 66% if the attorney takes a 40% contingency fee. If the client litigates individually and receives an award twenty percent higher than the settlement payout, he or she will net 80% of the settlement payout if the contingency fee is 33%, but only 72% of the settlement payout if the contingency fee is 40%.

The following table summarizes this arithmetic:

	GROSS SETTLEMENT	ATTORNEYS' FEE RATE	NET AWARD TO CLIENT	NET FEE TO ATTORNEY
UNDER THE GLOBAL SETTLEMENT	$ X ($7,500 - $75,000)	25%	75% of $ X	25% of $ X
INDIVIDUAL LITIGATION	$ X + 10%	33%	73% of $ X	37% of $ X
		40%	66% of $ X	44% of $ X
	$ X + 20%	33%	80% of $ X	40% of $ X
		40%	72% of $ X	48% of $ X

The table demonstrates that under some scenarios clients do better by opting out of the settlement, while in other scenarios they do not. In any event, the settlement number has been chosen so that clients do approximately as well in the settlement as out of it. The lawyers invariably do better in the individual litigation.

a) The point of this question is that the lawyers will do substantially better negotiating a "separate peace" for their inventory clients. If, for example, a lawyer charging a 40% contingency fee negotiates a settlement 20% better than the payout in the global settlement, that lawyer will net 48% of the global-settlement payout, rather than 25%. In other words, the lawyer does 92% better under the "separate peace" than under the global settlement. The client, by contrast, may do worse under the separate peace. To be concrete: for a stomach cancer, which the global settlement will compensate with $75,000, the lawyer gets $18,750 under the settlement but gets $36,000 negotiating a separate settlement of $90,000. However, the client would get $56,250 under the settlement, but would get only $54,000 under the individually-negotiated settlement. Points for discussion follow directly from the numbers. First, why should the class clients do worse than the inventory client? To this, the answer is reassuring: they don't really do worse. Although they get less money, they pay less in attorneys' fees, so their net is nearly the same. Second, what if some particular clients would do better under one scenario than under another? Thus, in the hypothetical just presented, the inventory client actually nets less under the individual settlement than under the global settlement. Third, can the attorney, who makes vastly more money negotiating a separate peace for the inventory clients, disentangle his or her personal interests from the class interests? Of course, the attorney will have some higher costs with individual recoveries but even so, for an attorney with thousands of inventory clients, the difference in fees might amount to millions.

b) The quick answer to Problem 8(b) is no. The lawyer cannot possibly represent the class, which was the *Amchem v. Windsor* argument. However, the consortium of plaintiffs' lawyers may well be able to represent the different subclasses, negotiating with each other as well as with the defendants. Even if class counsel would be embroiled in irreparable conflicts of interest if the case was litigated, the point of the settlement class action is to prevent litigation, so the conflict possibilities aren't the same. This point may be hard for students to grasp – it is actually hard for anyone to grasp.

Problem 8(c) raises one of the most controversial and hotly-criticized provisions of the *Georgine* settlement (although it was not one of the reasons that the Supreme Court voided that settlement). Can the settlement stipulate that you must counsel your future clients about the wisdom of not opting out? Arguably, this settlement provision violates Model Rule 5.6(b), "A lawyer shall not participate in offering or making an agreement in which a restriction on the lawyer's right to practice is part of the settlement of a controversy between private parties." Legal ethics experts differed widely on this question at the *Georgine* fairness hearing (a disagreement detailed in Professor Koniak's article cited in footnote 123). The settlement provision also arguably violates Model Rule 1.7(a)(2), "a lawyer shall not represent a client if...there is a significant risk that the representation of one or more clients will be materially limited by the lawyer's responsibilities to another client, a former client or a third person or by a personal interest of the lawyer." Here, all three conflicts are present. The lawyer's responsibilities to advise each client disinterestedly are limited by responsibilities to other clients, whose prospects may be damaged if the global settlement unravels because of too many opt-outs; by the lawyer's responsibilities to third parties (those with whom the lawyer has signed the settlement agreement); and by the lawyer's own interests in not having the settlement unravel. A major global settlement may mean staggering amounts of money for class counsel – the difference between "merely" owning a personal jet and owning a major-league baseball team.

The Vioxx problem is new in this edition, and raises further variations on these themes. None of the questions raised on page 670 have settled answers, and the Zipursky paper cited in note 138, from which we have drawn the questions, make no claim to offer an authoritative answer to them. (An abbreviated form of the argument may be found in a blog post: "Getting With the Program: The Vioxx Settlement Agreement," posting of Anthony Sebok & Benjamin Zipursky to Findlaw's Writ, http://writ.news.findlaw.com/commentary/20071120_zipursky.html, Nov. 20, 2007.) We are inclined to agree with Zipursky that traditional legal ethics principles may not permit an aggregate settlement structured like the Vioxx settlement. Working backward from question 5: We see no ground in Rule 1.16 that would permit the lawyer to withdraw to the client's detriment. If the lawyer cannot withdraw, then "Settle or you're fired!" (Question 1) is also impermissible. Likewise, if the lawyer cannot withdraw then the question of whether the agreement violates rule 5.6 is irrelevant. As for the other questions: we do not believe that the lawyer's advice to the client violates Rule 2.1 so long as the lawyer genuinely thinks the settlement is to all clients' advantage. For the same reason, the lawyer's advice is not materially limited in violation of Rule 1.7 if it is advice that the lawyer would give regardless of the agreement.

H. Fee-Related Conflicts of Interest

1. Conflicts in Public Interest Representation

Problem 10 raises related questions of lawyer accountability. It also poses an issue that has been inadequately addressed by courts, commentators, and ethics committees: the extent to which retainer agreements can limit attorneys' obligations. Some private firms and public interest organizations have attempted to respond to the situation posed in Problem 9(a) by asking pro bono clients to underwrite a part of litigation expenses. Some organizations have also adopted internal policies against waiving fees as a condition of settlement. Under Model Rule 1.2(c), a lawyer may limit the objectives of the representation if the client consents after consultation. Many organizations have retainer agreements providing either that the client will reject any settlement offer that requires a fee waiver, or will pay the lawyers' fees and costs out of the settlement. A question worth discussing is whether bar organizations or legislatures should seek a rule to prevent defendants from demanding such waivers. It is, however, worth noting that the practice is not always as unjustifiable as some students assume. For example, in suits against public institutions, if a fee award will come out of a fixed budget, and will consume funds otherwise available to support remedial initiatives, the request for waivers becomes more defensible.

Professors may wish to draw together *Jeff D.* and the *Buckhannon* decision. Each of them places a weapon in the hands of defendants in public interest cases. *Jeff D.* allows defendants to erode the resources of public interest lawyers by strategically offering their clients favorable settlements with no attorneys' fees, while *Buckhannon* allows them to remedy the situation and preempt fees after large sums have been spent on the litigation. As a practical matter, the risks are not as great for many public interest lawyers as the doctrine would allow. Governmental defendants are often sympathetic to the general objectives of the public interest bar and would like to be able to afford at least some of the relief requested. Many of these defendants have no desire to bankrupt their opponents or to jeopardize negotiations by insisting on a waiver. Unless the litigation becomes acrimonious or their budgets are extremely limited, these defendants will not seek to avoid paying reasonable attorneys fees, although disputes may arise about what is reasonable. That may explain why the Albiston and Nielson study cited on page 680, n.146 found that only a third of surveyed public interest organizations reported that *Bukhannon* had made their work more difficult. Another reason is that most public interest work does not involve litigation that permits fee shifting. Rhode's study of fifty of the nation's most prominent public interest organizations found that the mean proportion of their budgets that came from fees was only 8 percent and that fewer than 15 percent relied on fees for at least a fifth of their budgets. [8]

By discussing funding issues in public interest representation, we hope to encourage reflection about the profession's financial responsibilities toward pro bono work. We seek to leave students in our own classes with the view that public interest work is not simply a branch of practice but an obligation and opportunity for the entire bar.

2. Attorney Buyouts and Gag Orders

---

[8]Deborah L. Rhode, Public Interest Law: The Movement at Midlife,"60 *Stan. L. Rev.*2027, 2054 (2008).

Problem 11 raises a different kind of question about conflicts between client, attorney, and public interests. What should an attorney do if the only way to maximize the client's interest is by negotiating a settlement that keeps valuable "public goods," such as information about health and safety hazards, or even the attorney's own expertise, out of reach of the public? This problem offers a good way to teach the otherwise-obscure Model Rule 5.6; it also raises an issue that is currently the subject of intense controversy. Professors should note that Florida and Texas have both enacted rules greatly restricting secret settlements and gag orders.[9] The Texas rule, for example, creates a "presumption of openness" of court records to the general public, and permits records to be sealed only by "a specific, serious and substantial interest which clearly outweighs . . . this presumption of openness." Courts must consider "any probable adverse effect that sealing will have upon the general public health or safety" and must consider whether there are no less restrictive means than secrecy to safeguard the parties' objectives. Significantly, court records include not only officially filed records, but also "settlement agreements not filed of record" and "discovery, not filed of record" if either concerns "matters that have a probable adverse effect upon the general public health or safety, or the administration of public office, or the operation of government, except discovery in cases originally initiated to preserve bona fide trade secrets or other intangible property rights." Hearings on any motion to seal court records are public and require public notice; and non-parties have a right to intervene.

Since many students are understandably disturbed by confidential settlements, it may be appropriate to amplify some of the arguments in their defense. A Note in the 2003 *Georgetown Journal of Legal Ethics* Symposium on secret settlements points out that the vast majority of cases seeking to unseal documents are brought by the mass media. Defendants who are tried in the press on the basis of allegations that have never been proven may suffer substantial losses. A case in point occurred when CBS' 60 Minutes ran a story on the Audi 500 automobile, claiming that a sudden acceleration defect had resulted in numerous

---

[9] Sunshine in Litigation Act, Fla. Stat. ch. 69.081 (1990); Tex R. Civ. P. rule 76a.

deadly injuries. American consumers stopped buying, and the car was removed from the market, although subsequent investigation attributed the deaths to driver error rather than product defects.[10] On the other hand, the risks of allowing secrecy agreements are well illustrated by other recent cases noted in the text. The most prominent examples, also discussed in the *Georgetown Journal of Legal Ethics* Symposium, involved the Catholic Church, which insisted on secrecy agreements without assurances that the priests who engaged in sexual molestation would be removed from positions that endangered children.

3. Consumer Class Actions

This section discusses practices that many find outrageous. It is helpful in discussing these issues to distinguish two different criticisms. The first is that class counsel often receive substantial amounts of money while their clients receive very little. In many cases, however, individual class members may have suffered only minimal injuries. The primary function of the class action in these contexts is to deter wrongdoing that would not justify individual suits. The second criticism is that class lawyers negotiate settlements with favorable fee arrangements at the expense of clients. Here, the complaint is not just that the class members' recoveries are small, but that their recoveries are smaller than they would be if the attorney was not colluding with the defendant to line his or her own pocket. That is a violation of Rule 1.7(b); and, if Professors Cohen and Koniak are right, it may be outright fraud.

---

[10] Heather Waldbeser & Heather DeGrave, A Plaintiff's Lawyer's Dilemma: The Ethics of Entering a Confidential Settlement," 16 *Geo. J. L. Ethics* 815, 817 (2003).

A colorful recent class action involving " Hidden Sex Scenes" is an amusing case to explore whether litigation that benefits primarily attorneys also serves a useful deterrent value. In that case, involving the video game *Grand Theft Auto: San Andreas*, a civil lawsuit was filed after Congressional debate and on-line publicity drew attention to sex scenes, accessible only to knowledgeable players using special software. The game was rated as "adults only," but the suit charged fraud for failure to disclose the sex scenes. Some 2,676 buyers filed claims, which would be resolved under the settlement for $5 to $35 each, and in some instances, a sanitized copy of the game. The settlement was challenged by Theodore Frank, director of the Legal Center for the Public Interest at the American Enterprise Institute, who claimed that the suit had no merit. The plaintiffs responded that Frank had no standing to challenge the agreement because he had not alleged that he was offended by the scenes and therefore had no stake in the suit. They also maintained, amazingly enough, that if the suit was without merit, that made the settlement even more impressive.[11]

Rhode's *In the Interest of Justice* provides an overview of other examples of abuse and proposed remedies. Promising strategies include greater use of informed client steering committees, competition among potential class counsel, and special masters to review fee requests that seem out of proportion to the time expended and results achieved.

I. Other Conflicts of Interest

We conclude this chapter by briefly surveying several other areas of potential conflicts of interests: business relationships between lawyers and clients, media contracts, the advocate-witness rule, and lawyers in family relationships with other lawyers.

Problem 12 concerns business relationships between attorneys and clients. It raises controversial questions about the role of counsel who are also corporate officers. It also highlights a business practice of

---

[11] Jonathan D. Glater, "Game's Hidden Sex Scenes Draw Ho-Hum, Except From Lawyers," *N.Y. Times,* June 25, 2008, at C1.

attorneys taking fees in the form of client stock, a practice that began gaining prominence during the high-technology "bubble" of the late 1990s, when Silicon Valley lawyers became (sometimes briefly) dot-com multi-millionaires by brokering "marriages" between entrepreneurs and venture capitalists.

a) Under prevailing interpretations of the Model Rule 1.8, the arrangement described in the problem is acceptable – provided, of course, that the Rule's three conditions are met. The most difficult to interpret is 1.8(a)(1): how do the attorney and client determine whether the terms are fair? This question is closely connected with part (b). In teaching part (a), professors may vary the facts by making the attorney request compensation in the form of stock, rather than by having the client suggest it. Some highly influential Silicon Valley lawyers have reportedly insisted on receiving some portion of their fees in stock as a condition of representation.

b) Here the possible conflict is an important but subtle one. During negotiations between the clients and the venture capitalist, it is in the clients' interest that the fair market value of the shares be set as high as possible, in order to get the most capital. But it is in the attorney's interest to have the fair market value set as low as possible in order to get more shares for his fee. However, both sides are constrained by the desire to maintain mutual trust and a good working relationship, and to settle on terms that would not strike other investors as unreasonable.

c) There is no settled answer to this problem. Under Model Rule 1.7(b), the attorney must point out the possible conflicts of interest and obtain informed consent in writing.

d) Model Rule 1.8(c) prohibits lawyers from preparing instruments giving themselves gifts but a lawyer would hardly be likely to draft a golden parachute provision without ensuring that it could not technically be characterized as a gift. The question for class discussion is whether these formalities are enough to stop a generous parachute from being considered a gift. A prudent attorney would make sure that some other lawyer drafted the provision. It is worth noting that Daylian Cain, a professor of behavioral economics at Yale's School of Management, has demonstrated the unconscious ways that self- interest biases decisions relevant to conflicts of interest. In one of his experimental studies, auditors hired to assess the value of company being sold gave different valuations depending on their employment relationship. Sellers' auditors valued the company at a rate 30 percent higher than the buyers' auditors. All insisted that their role had nothing to do with estimate.

Media Contracts

In teaching this issue – which warrants only a few minutes of class time – professors may wish to use the retainer agreement in the *Maxwell* case cited in the text. (It is reproduced in full in *Maxwell v. Superior Court of Los Angeles,* 161 Cal. Rptr. 849, 852 (1980):

"IT IS HEREBY DISCLOSED BY THE LAWYERS TO MAXWELL that the provisions of this agreement may create a conflict of interest between Maxwell and the Lawyers, and that the provisions of this agreement may give to the Lawyers a monetary interest adverse to the interests of Maxwell. This conflict of interest may manifest itself in many ways including but not limited to the following: [P] a. The Lawyers may have an interest to create publicity which would increase the money which they might get as a result of this agreement, even if this publicity hurt Maxwell's defense. [P] b. The Lawyers may have an interest not to raise certain defenses which would questions the sanity or mental capacity of Maxwell because to raise these defenses might make this agreement between the Lawyers and Maxwell void or voidable by Maxwell. [P] c. The Lawyers may have an interest in having Maxwell be convicted and even sentenced to death so that there would be increased publicity which might mean that the Lawyers would get more money as a result of this agreement. [P] d. The Lawyers may have other interests which are adverse to Maxwell's interests as a result of this agreement. The Lawyers affirm that they will not be influenced in any way by any interest which may be adverse to that of Maxwell. The Lawyers will raise every defense which they, in their best judgment based upon their experience feel is warranted by the evidence and information at their disposal and which, taking into consideration the flow of trial and trial tactics, is in Maxwell's best interests. The Lawyers will conduct all aspects of the defense of Maxwell as would a reasonably competent attorney acting as a diligent, conscientious advocate."

Attorney-Client Sexual Relations

Unsurprisingly, the issue of lawyer-client sexual relationships can provoke interesting class disputes.

Prior to enactment of Model Rule 1.8(j), thirteen states had amended their ethics rules to include provisions concerning sexual relations. For example, the Florida rule as modified prohibits sexual relationships involving "exploitation": New York bans all sexual relationships in matters involving domestic relations. Critics of the Model Rule approach claim that it is both overinclusive (because it denies women's capacity to provide informed consent) and underinclusive (because it does not prevent attorneys from representing clients with whom they have had prior sexual relationships, which may be just as prejudicial).[12] A further criticism is that Model Rule 1.8(j) does not define "sexual relations," and leaves open whether more than one contact or sexual intercourse is required. As a practical matter, however, such concerns may be overstated. The cases in which bar complaints have been filed almost always involve egregious conduct, and given their frequency, a bright-line approach has much to recommend it.

Problem 13 is useful not only for discussing the constitutional issue it raises explicitly, but also for analyzing the bar's rationale for Rule 1.8(j) and eliciting student reactions to a rule that appears to be – for better or for worse – quite paternalistic. Please note that we have deliberately refrained from specifying the gender of Lawyers A and B in the problem, to leave it open whether the relationship is heterosexual or

---

[12] Philip R. Bowers and Tanya E. Stern, "Conflict of Interest?: The Absolute Ban on Lawyer-Client Sexual Relationships Is Not Absolutely Necessary," 16 *Geo. J. Legal Ethics* 535, 542-48 (2003).

homosexual; professors may vary the hypothetical as they wish.

In analyzing the constitutional issue, perhaps the central question is whether Rule 1.8(j), like the Texas statute in *Lawrence*, "furthers no state interest which can justify its intrusion into the personal and private life of the individual." The question is whether the bar is entitled to prohibit lawyer-client sexual relationships in advance (professors should probably avoid using the term "prophylactic regulation" in this context; the double entendres arising from "inside counsel" are already bad enough) or whether lawyers can only be disciplined after the fact if they abuse the fiduciary relationship. Oddly enough, the most relevant Supreme Court precedents are probably the two solicitation cases *Ohralik* (included in Chapter XII, section B) and *Edenfield v. Fane*, 507 U.S. 761 (1993). *Ohralik* upheld prophylactic anti-solicitation rules in situations where overreaching by lawyers poses a danger and the goal is pecuniary gain. *Edenfield* struck down similar rules pertaining to accountants, distinguishing the cases in part because a lawyer, unlike an accountant, is "a professional trained in the art of persuasion." *Edenfield*, 507 U.S. at 775, quoting *Ohralik*. Presumably, the dangers of overreaching by "a professional trained in the art of persuasion" are present in a seduction – a sexual solicitation – just as in a solicitation of a client. This suggests that a rule forbidding attorney-client sexual relationships might be upheld on the same ground that *Ohralik* offered for the rule against in-person solicitation. On the other hand, it seems quite possible that the ban on attorney-client sex in the corporate context would not survive constitutional scrutiny.

CHAPTER XI: LAWYER-CLIENT DECISION MAKING

Chapter XI focuses on the problem of paternalistic behavior by lawyers toward their clients. In everyday conversation, to describe someone as "paternalistic" is generally to imply a character flaw. It suggests someone at once overbearing and condescending, albeit out of benevolent motivations. Our analysis uses the term in a more precise sense, stripped of its negative connotations. "Paternalism" in this discussion means interfering with another's liberty for his or her own good. In this sense, paternalism may under some circumstances be justified – restraining an absent-minded pedestrian who is about to step in front of a speeding truck is surely an example of justified paternalism – and that is why the term should initially be regarded as value-neutral. It will probably be necessary to emphasize this point to students, who almost always assume that paternalism is wrong. It is not hard to see why: Given our society's enormous commitment to freedom of choice, we would view many instances of even well-intentioned interference with suspicion. A person who habitually treats others paternalistically undermines their autonomy, which is why paternalism has acquired its negative connotations.

Doing It Quickly

This chapter is short enough that teachers can assign it in its entirety, even though they may not take class time to discuss every reading. The chapter teaches very well from the problems, though professors may wish to choose between Problems 3 and 4, since they raise similar issues. Alternatively, it is possible to substitute the *Kaczynski* Unabomber case – with its eloquent dissent by Judge Reinhardt – for Problem 1. Professors who wish to cover the chapter in a single two-hour class could spend the first hour on *Jones v. Barnes*, Model Rule 1.2(a), and either *Kaczynski* or Problem 1. In the second hour, discussion could focus on Problems 3 and/or 4, together with the accompanying readings and Model Rule 1.14. The most important question raised by the Rule is what it means to "maintain a normal client-lawyer relationship with the client," if the lawyer fears that following the client's instructions will be injurious to his or her interests.

The problem of the death row defendant who wants to die is likely to spark an important debate. For those sympathetic to Gilmore's demand that the ACLU "butt out of my life and butt out of my death," the ACLU's response is instructive. According to the Garnett article cited in the footnote, part of what motivates lawyers to oppose the death penalty despite their clients' wishes is the belief that their clients are "irrational and depressed." However, those concerns are often "makeweights." The far stronger motivation is to prevent an immoral punishment.[1]

It is helpful to review Rita's Case from the Introduction in connection with this chapter. One possible reading of that case is as follows. Gladys, Rita's grandmother, wanted not only custody of Rita, but also back-up help from social services agencies whenever she found the responsibilities too difficult. Her attorneys, immediately realizing that she wanted something that the legal system would not readily give, unconsciously translated her need into one that the legal system *could* fulfill: adopting Rita. ("When your only tool is a hammer, the whole world is a nail" is an apt metaphor.) At the end of Rita's Case, it is far from clear that their "victory" has given Gladys what she needs or wants, rather than an approximation that her attorneys believed they could achieve.

Jones v. Barnes

Jones v. Barnes clearly displays the moral principles underlying the debate over paternalism. The majority believes that lawyers should be free to ignore clients' tactical suggestions, because the lawyer knows better than the client what will work. By contrast, the dissent repeatedly emphasizes the importance of client autonomy and dignity. A key issue concerns Barnes' motivation in asking Melinger to present certain arguments on appeal. Was he simply trying to second-guess his lawyer tactically, as the majority supposes, or did he wish those arguments raised as a matter of principle? The discussion questions are intended: (a) to highlight the differences between the outcome-oriented approach of the majority and the due process emphasis on human dignity by the dissent; (b) to suggest that neither principle should be taken to the limit;

---

[1] Richard W. Garnett, "Sectarian Reflections on Lawyers' Ethics and Death Row Volunteers." 77 *Notre Dame L. Rev.* 795, 811 (2002).

and (c) to raise the practical question of how a lawyer can tell whether making a certain legal argument is central to a client's dignity or attorney.

United States v. Kaczynski

The Unabomber case is straightforward to teach. Judge Reinhardt's dissenting opinion makes it excruciatingly clear that Kaczynski's last-minute demand to represent himself pro se was a desperate maneuver to prevent his lawyers from presenting a mental illness defense, and that he accepted the plea bargain for the same reason. It is noteworthy that Judge Reinhardt also personally believes that Kaczynski should not have been permitted to represent himself, but he is correct that *Faretta* requires otherwise.

The key question is why Kaczynski's lawyers insisted on presenting a defense that he found totally unacceptable. Perhaps they truly believed he was incompetent – but professors might well ask whether lawyers should feel free to disregard desires that are so strongly felt, even if the client is not fully rational. The note material in Question 1 presents Michael Mello's forceful argument that Kaczynski was not insane – that he was something perhaps more disquieting: a sane but thoroughly evil individual. If Mello is right, then shouldn't Clarke and Denvir have regarded Kaczynski's desire not to be portrayed to millions of people as a "grotesque and repellant lunatic" as one of his objectives in the representation – which, under Model Rule 1.2(a), it is up to Kaczynski to determine?

Question 4. According to Monroe Freedman, the client should have the right to determine how his defense should proceed in the World Trade Center bombing case. However, whether the lawyer violated that right is not entirely clear, and Freedman concludes his decision with one possible scenario:

> Lawyer: Your only chance of getting off is to let the jury know that you were a dupe and that the real bad guy was your leader.
>
> Client: You're out of your mind. They'd probably kill me if I said that.

165

Lawyer: Then what if we do it this way? I'll argue to the jury that you were just a dupe, and you'll tell your friends that you can't believe your ears, that I totally changed everything that you and I agreed on.

Client: Sounds good to me. Let's do that.

I don't know whether that's what happened, but it wouldn't be the first time that a lawyer took the heat for a client. Ironically, one of the reasons that lawyers have never been high in public esteem is that we do that job – taking the heat for the client – so well.[2]

Problem 2

Students are likely to find Problem 2 troubling, because their reflexive anti-paternalistic stance seems to suggest that they should assist a double suicide. They are likely to grasp at the suggestion that Model Rules 1.2(d) and 1.6 resolve their problem, at which point the professor should point out that with careful planning the two partners can make their suicides perfectly lawful in jurisdictions that forbid assisting suicide but not suicide itself.

In the actual case, the clients stated that they planned to take sedatives and then poison themselves with carbon monoxide by running their car in a closed garage. After considerable soul-searching, their lawyers chose to write the wills. The lawyers

had to make a call, and did so by determining that suicide wasn't a crime; by determining that by staying in the car, the passenger who didn't turn the ignition key would be committing unassisted suicide; by adhering to the nondisclosure dictate in the rules; and by applying a personal conviction that an individual has a right to commit suicide.

---

[2] Monroe Freedman, "Whose Case Is It Anyway?", *Legal Times*, March 28, 1994.

About two weeks passed between the initial appointment and the day the wills were signed. Another week or two later, the two lawyers saw their clients' story on the front page of the local newspaper.

According to news reports, the clients had taken pills, then sat in the car in their Piscataway garage as a hose attached to the exhaust pipe ran carbon monoxide into the vehicle. The ill partner eventually awoke, went into the house and found his companion dead of a self-inflicted shotgun blast. He then attempted to kill himself by slitting his wrists. When that failed, he called the police.

Prosecutors determined that no crime had been committed. [The lawyer] says he was never approached by the prosecutor's office to discuss his office's representation of the two men. The surviving partner later moved out of state, and has since died....[3]

We also include materials on the moral justification of paternalism, focusing on four approaches. The first is Dennis Thompson's proposal of certain objective conditions for justified paternalism (client incompetence, severe and irreversible damage if the client makes the wrong choice, and minimal interference with client liberty). The second is Gerald Dworkin's hypothetical consent test (what would an ideally rational client want?). A third is Duncan Kennedy's ad hoc approach (based on empathy with the client). The final approach is David Luban's suggestion that paternalism can be justified if it is in the service of the client's own deeply-held values, which are occasionally threatened by strong emotion or a weak will.

C. Informed Consent

The chapter next discusses informed consent. In our experience, many students assume that such consent is a simple solution to problems of paternalism. To counteract this tendency, the notes stress

---

[3] Richard Pliskin, "The Ethics of Suicide," *N. J. L. J.*, June 20, 1994, at 1.

the enormous practical difficulties involved in presenting information neutrally and comprehensibly, as well as the difficulties in avoiding manipulation.

This discussion leads directly to issues of when clients are competent to give informed consent. In some cases, clients with no obvious physical infirmities may nevertheless express such odd preferences that their attorneys are likely to regard them as incompetent. The notes explore Duncan Kennedy's suggestion that lawyers should rely on empathy to decide whether the client is competent and compare this approach with a test of competence drawn from a nineteenth century estates case. That case involved the attempt by relatives to invalidate an elderly man's will. It is worthwhile to ask students how this test would resolve the various problems, examples, and hypotheticals in the chapter. They will discover that the test does not find very much behavior to be incompetent, and for this reason many will search for a less restrictive alternative.

Problems 3 and 4

These problems are quite straightforward to teach. We have discovered in discussions of Problem 3 that students differ widely over when a child reaches the "age of reason" and is entitled to dictate the objectives of representation. Lawyers, too, will differ. Jean Koh Peters, who has written a major treatise on the legal representation of children, has stated that she will follow the instructions of clients as young as six, even if she regards their preferences as self-destructive. Quoting that view is likely to provoke a good discussion. Other juvenile rights' lawyers whom we have consulted stress that minors who are given full information about their options are generally no less able than adults in similar circumstances to make reasoned choices. The most common problem is that the options are so often inadequate. The *Fordham Law Review* (vol. 64) Symposium cited in footnotes 96-98 offers a comprehensive exploration of issues involved in representing juveniles.

The Ethics 2000 Commission's modifications of Rule 1.14 are also worth noting. The old Rule's references to "client under disability" were changed to "client with diminished capacity" in order to convey the continuum of a client's impairment. The most important modification is language providing that where the lawyer believes that a client with diminished capacity is at risk of physical, financial, or other harm unless action is taken, the lawyer may take necessary protective action. Such action may include requesting appointment of a guardian or revealing confidences impliedly authorized under Rule 1.6 to carry out the representation.

The law student's poignant case-history (pp. 751-753) is also an extremely effective teaching tool. His observation that t A.B.'s mother "pointed out how the system has failed and pointed out my role in that" leads to an especially powerful concluding paragraph.

Problem 4

We end the chapter with a problem in which the client is not weak, poor, uneducated, very young, or very old. Our point is to emphasize that even powerful, self-confident, and successful individuals can suffer from bad judgment. The message is that all lawyers, whatever their practice speciality, are likely to face problems of paternalism.

CHAPTER XII: REGULATING THE MARKET

This chapter begins with an overview of reasons for regulating the market for legal services. The introductory material offers an economic focus. Professors may also wish to question whether non-economic factors such as concerns about commercialism and the bar's status as a profession rather than a business should play a role in shaping regulatory policy.

Doing It Quickly

One possible allocation of time would be as follows: one classroom hour each for advertising, solicitation, unauthorized practice, and lawyers' fees. If time permits, it is also possible to combine the section on acquiring an interest in litigation with lawyers' fees. The material in Section G on the creative financing of lawsuits and in Section E on multidisciplinary practice is interesting and timely , but could be omitted or condensed for brief discussion.

The longest section of the chapter is that on solicitation. Professors aiming to reduce the reading assignment should consider assigning only the *Ohralik*, *Primus*, and *Teichner* cases, together with the notes and questions. Sections C and D could also be omitted.

A. Advertising

Problem 1 provides a good overview of controversies surrounding advertising restrictions. Discussion could focus on:

a) the absence of information about what the claim was or why it was successful;

b) the ambiguity of the quoted terms and whether anyone is likely to be misled by such puffing;

c) the failure to specify what is a "reasonable" fee or what is a "routine" case;

d) the ambiguities and problems of substantiation

surrounding what constitutes a discount; the ambiguity of the boast (maybe it means "the best possible settlement given that I'm going to do it as quickly as possible," when a better settlement could be obtained by a lawyer who was willing to spend time on the case); and the misleading suggestion that there is anything unusual about a trial lawyer settling most cases;[1]

e) the omission of other potentially material information such as how many drunk driving charges the firm has failed to get thrown out;

f)   the lack of relevant information conveyed by testimonials and "unjustified expectations" about winning;[2]

---

[1] In *Matter of Wamsley*, 725 N. E. 2nd 75 (2000) the court found that these statements implied something excessive about the quality of the lawyer's services and "likely created an unjustified expectation" of the results that he could achieve. The court publicly admonished the lawyer for his conduct.

[2] In *Oring v. State Bar of California*, appeal dismissed, 488 U.S. 590 (1989), the Supreme Court heard oral argument in a case barring client testimonials. The Court then summarily dismissed the case for want of a properly presented federal question after California amended its rules to permit testimonials accompanied by a disclaimer such as "this endorsement does not constitute a guarantee, warranty or

g) through l), the concerns about professional dignity.

Nathan Koppell's article ,"Objection! Funny Legal Ads Draw Censure," *Wall St. J.*, Feb 8, 2008, details a number of advertising controversies that also make for engaging discussion, including New York's ban on a TV ad showing lawyers representing space aliens who had crashed their flying saucer, South Carolina's debate over bans on "showmanship, puffery, or huckusterism," and Florida's varying decisions on animals: panthers have been approved, but not sharks, pit bulls or tigers. Banning an ad depicting a pit bull, the Florida Supreme Court reasoned that "Were we to approve the referee's finding, images of sharks, wolves, crocodiles, and piranhas could follow." Fla. Bar v. Pape, 918 So.2d 240, 247 (Fla. 2005). "Lions," according to Public Citizen Lawyer Gary Beck, "are an open question." They can be both "vicious and noble" and the controversy is "kafkaesque."

A good class discussion is also possible on more general questions about advertising regulation. Students on opposite ends of the ideological spectrum may find commercialism distasteful but disagree about how to respond to it. The ABA's Commission report, *Lawyer Advertising at a Crossroads: Professional Policy Considerations* (1995) provides a good overview of the issues.

---

prediction regarding the outcome of your legal matter."

172

Many state bar commissions on professionalism have lamented tasteless advertising; other bar leaders have responded in kind. An irony worth noting is that the limerick in Problem 1 (I) was part of an Ohio State Bar Association campaign, while its code of conduct prohibited undignified advertisements.[3] Similarly, a Tucson lawyer who opposes lawyer advertising has subsidized a campaign featuring television and billboard ads that maintain: "The Lawyer You're Looking for Isn't on T.V."[4] So, too, elite attorneys who object to mass marketing are increasingly resorting to proactive public relations strategies, internet profiles, and promotional literature described in articles such as "Hawking Legal Services" and "Finetuning a Newsletter."[5] Some firms are bankrolling image campaigns, complete with corporate logos (bulldogs, jungle cats – but presumably not in Florida!) and humorous print ads (e.g., "research shows Lather and Gage clients tell 73% fewer lawyer jokes at parties").[6]

---

[3] Andrews, "The Selling of a Precedent," *Student Law.*, March, 1982 at 12, 49.

[4] "The Billboard Wars," *Legal Reformer*, Jan.-Mar., 1990, at 9.

[5] Reynoldson, "The Case Against Lawyer Advertising," *A.B.A. J.*, Jan., 1989, at 61.

[6] Richard B. Schmitt, Lawyers Try In-Your-Face Punches," *Wall St. J.* Jan. 12, 2001 at B1, B5. Students can ponder whether bar officials could find this ad misleading.

The problems created by internet advertising are also worth exploring. Recent estimates suggest that a majority of the nation's attorneys have on-line listings. And as a *Wall Street Journal* article noted: "For unscrupulous lawyers, the Web is the perfect marketing tool–cheap, pervasive, and lacking serious regulation."[7]

Web sites enable attorneys to make misleading claims and to reach clients in jurisdictions where they are not licensed. The *Wall Street Journal* cites some chilling examples. For example, a dot-com conglomerate whose main business is selling transmission repair and maid service franchises, also runs an online referral service that matches lawyers and clients. The site, which claims to offer "the best hand-picked, consumer-rated lawyers on the planet" includes a California lawyer who in 1998 completed a 42-month suspension in connection with a federal conviction for defrauding his ex-wife in a bankruptcy proceeding. State bars generally lacks sufficient resources to screen web listings. The challenge involved in regulating internet communications can be taken up again in the discussion of unauthorized practice of law and multijurisdictional practice.

B. Solicitation

These materials offer competing perspectives on solicitation. The rationale for the bar's traditional policy is set forth in *Ohralik*, and the abuses that have served to justify such a policy are illustrated by *Ohralik*. Competing interests in facilitating access to legal services appear in the excerpts from Auerbach and *Primus*.

In his dissent in *Primus*, Justice Rehnquist warns that "the next lawyer in Ohralik's shoes who is disciplined for similar conduct will come here cloaked in the prescribed mantle of 'political association' to assure that insurance companies do not take unfair advantage of policyholders." His words were prescient: *Teichner* appears to be that case, given that Marshall Teichner was working for a fee, not pro bono. The question *Teichner* poses is whether the courts have been focusing

---

[7] Richard B. Schmitt, "Lawyers Flood Web, But Many Ads Fail to Tell Whole Truth," *Wall St. J.* Jan. 15, 2001, at A1.

on the right question. Should the issue be whether Teichner took a fee and was affiliated with a community organization, or whether his conduct met reasonable time, place, and manner standards and whether he provided effective representation?

Problems 2 and 3

Most of the practices in Problems 2 and 3 are impermissible. Class discussion can focus on whether they should be. In Problem 3(b) and (c), if the lawyer didn't initiate personal contact with anyone, he may not be in violation of ethical rules.

A critical question is whether a less restrictive approach to solicitation would be appropriate. This issue arises naturally from question 3 following the reading. If the state can realize its objective of preventing lawyer overreaching by a less restrictive approach than in the Code or Model Rules, *Central Hudson* suggests that these rules violate the First Amendment. It is worth noting that traditional exceptions to the ban on solicitation have included contacts with friends, relatives, and existing clients, which shield most personal marketing activities of corporate lawyers, but fail to address the needs of other segments of the profession. A useful recurring question to pose is whether distinctions based on attorneys' motives are sufficiently attentive to societal interests in maximizing information available to clients.

Professors may also wish to explore a potential collision-course that some observers have detected between the Supreme Court's advertising and solicitation cases. The progress from generalized advertising (as in *Bates*) to targeted advertising (*Zauderer*) to targeted direct mailings (*Shapero*) has established powerful limits on bar regulation of truthful advertising, even if it is directed at particular groups. At the same time, *Ohralik* and *Went For It* establish that regulation of for-profit solicitation is constitutionally permissible. The collision course arises because the two practices begin to converge. If, for example, a lawyer mails a DVD to a potential client, is that advertising or solicitation? What about personalized Internet contact? These are, as yet, relatively uncharted waters.

Problems in enforcement are also worth exploring. In a case

involving attorneys who allegedly appeared at wakes and funerals for victims of a school bus crash, the local district attorney observed that "some lawyers have the attitude of 'If become a millionaire, I don't care if they take my license.'"[8] Professors may ask students whether criminal prosecution or invalidation of retainer agreements would provide sufficient protection in those circumstances?.

A related issue is how best to enforce rules prohibiting lawyers from compensating non-lawyers who refer cases. The rationale for that prohibition is that any alternative approach would encourage third parties to recommend attorneys based on the size of kickbacks rather than the quality of services. It is useful to question how effectively this rule can be enforced where the compensation consists of personal favors rather than cash.

---

[8] Kennedy, "Grief, Greed and the Lawyers," *Los Angeles Times*, May 29, 1980 at E 1 (quoting Rene Guerra). *See also* Belkin, "Where 21 Youths Died, Lawyers Wage a War," *N.Y. Times*, Jan. 18, 1990, at A15 (noting allegations that one lawyer attached a retainer contract to a condolence card and another promised to help subsidize purchase of a new home).

C. Specialization and Group Legal Services

Depending on student interest, professors may wish to skim this material or to assign it later in connection with Chapter XV's discussion of competence. We felt it was important to provide a summary of the debate surrounding state specialization programs since current trends within the bar make the issue unlikely to disappear. One current question, noted in Chapter III's discussion of bar regulatory codes, is whether specialty organizations such as the American Academy of Matrimonial Lawyers could be a vehicle for developing desirable practice-specific standards.

The material on group legal services and referral plans is designed to raise questions about the appropriate scope of bar regulation. Current disciplinary rules would prohibit the consumer organization's plan if the organization is for profit. They would also ban the proposed referral service if the sponsoring organization is run by lawyers for their financial benefit or if it derives any profit from the rendition of services. Such restrictions have frequently been criticized by commentators as unjustified barriers to the delivery of legal services. Model Rule 7.2 prohibits for-profit lawyer referral services and the accompanying commentary does not attempt to justify that prohibition. The Model Rules would not, however, ban the for-profit consumer organization plan. A central question to consider is whether restrictions on group or referral services run for profit are appropriate as long as there is no organizational interference with individual lawyer-client relationships. Similar issues arise concerning multidisciplinary practice. The question briefly raised about Internet referral services, is likely to assume increasing importance and to hold interest for many students.

D. Unauthorized Practice of Law: Nonlawyer Services and Multijurisdictional Practice

The materials on unauthorized practice raise issues about the appropriate scope and oversight of restrictions on lay competition. What underlies the bar's opposition to such competition? To what extent is that opposition motivated by concerns about status and money, and to what extent by concerns about consumer injury? Students can also consider how they would respond as members of the ABA or the Commission or an analogous state bar task force considering changes in unauthorized practice rules. The *Brumbaugh* case lends itself well to role-playing; students can act as counsel both for Brumbaugh and the bar.

In addition, professors can pursue doctrinal issues concerning the definition of legal practice. A survey of newspaper advice columns will often yield examples of lay advice. Rhode's example of Marcus Arnold draws on Michael Lewis's best-seller *Next: The Future Just Happened* (2001) and in a *New York Times Magazine* article based on the book.[9] Lewis writes:

---

[9] Michael Lewis, "Faking It," *NY Times Mag.*, July 15, 2001, at 32.

The knowledge gap between lawyers and nonlawyers had been shrinking for some time, and the Internet was closing it further. Legal advice was being supplied over the Internet, often free – and it wasn't just lawyers doing the supplying. Students, cops, dicks, even ex-cons went onto message boards to help people with their questions and cases. At the bottom of this phenomenon was a corrosively democratic attitude toward legal knowledge, which the legal profession now simply took for granted. "If you think about the law," the co-chairman of the American Bar Association task force on "e-lawyering," Richard S. Granat, said in an interview in *The New York Times*, in an attempt to explain the boom in do-it-yourself Internet legal services, "a large component is just information. Information by itself can go a long way to help solve legal problems."[10]

Lewis adds: "In that simple sentence you could hear whatever was left of the old professional mystique evaporating."

The Internet has led to other changes that make traditional unauthorized practice seem increasingly anachronistic. The evolution of self-help web sites, including some run by bar associations, have increased consumers' interest in pro se representation and their resistance to barriers that stand in the way.[11] And the global reach of information provided by lawyers over the Net makes prohibitions on out-of-state practitioners harder to enforce or justify.

Herbert Kritzer points out that professionals in law, as in other fields, have helped to create many of the conditions that invite greater lay competition and build demand for competitors' services. Innovations designed to increase efficiency by routinizing tasks and delegating them to non-professionals have also enabled independent providers to offer cost-effective services in a growing number of fields. And as Kritzer notes, when "previously restricted tasks have been opened to new

---

[10] Id.

[11] Caitlin Liu, "Aided by the Internet, Self-Help Law Matures," *L. A. Times*, Aug 10, 2001, at A2. (describing bar association Web sites in Arizona, California, Connecticut, Hawaii, and New Jersey).

providers, the problems predicted by the profession opposing relaxation of restriction have failed to materialize in significant numbers (if at all)."[12]

Questions to explore are how the bar and courts should respond to such increased demand for lay services and whether the definition of legal practice can have content that is not circular or conclusory. It is important to point out that current prohibitions usually encompass activities of other licensed vocational groups, such as accountants or real estate brokers. Given the absence of evidence suggesting that lawyers' competence and ethical standards are substantially higher than members of such occupations, students should consider whether traditional definitions of unauthorized practice require reassessment.

The issues of multijurisdictional practice, GATS, and outsourcing are assuming greater importance in a world of increasingly national and global legal practice. Among the key issues are how much autonomy the profession should have in making decisions about what services can be performed by lawyers not licensed in a particular jurisdiction. One question that can spark interesting class discussion is when clients must be consulted about outsourcing.

E. Multidisciplinary Practice

---

[12] Kritzer, "The Professions Are Dead, Long Live the Professions: Legal Practice in a Post-Professional World," 33 *Law & Society Rev.* 713 (1999), at 728.

The debates over multidisciplinary practice offer another opportunity for raising basic questions about the meaning of professionalism. Both proponents and opponents of diversification represent powerful constituencies within the bar, and their debates have become quite heated. Jerald Solovy, a member of the ABA Litigation Section's Ancillary Business Committee captured the tone of some discussions in his observation that "this stuff stinks." In his view, the argument for these business dealings is, "in short, hokum. We're not a supermarket, we're a law firm and we should stay in the profession of law."[13] Proponents for their part often dismiss opposition concerns as unsupported or anachronistic. The issue lends itself to role-playing and the articles cited in the notes offer useful background for a debate.

The debate about MDP has become one of the most active in the practicing bar and professional responsibility scholarship. This is, in large part, a response to the encroachment of the Big Four accounting firms on traditional law-firm territory. The ABA Commission on Multidisciplinary Practice reported that by 1998 two of the four biggest legal services providers in the world were accounting firms. The potent combination of globalization and the permissibility of MDP in Europe has made the threat (or promise) of MDP a high-temperature issue for American law firms, particularly as they compete with accounting firms to hire law graduates. Professors who devote class time to the MDP issue should be sensitive to the possibility that some third-year students may have already opted for a multidisciplinary law practice.

New York has pioneered an alternative to full-fledged multidisciplinary practice. Its recently amended ethical rules that permit "contractual relationships" between lawyers and nonlawyers who wish to offer integrated legal and nonlegal services. This is the first state authorization of MDP. The New York regulatory structure:

- imposes minimum educational standards on nonlawyer

---

[13] Gibbons, "Branching Out," 75 *A.B.A. J.* 73 (1989) (quoting Solovy).

professionals seeking to participate in strategic alliances with lawyers and requires them to be licensed by a government entity and bound by an enforceable code of ethical conduct;

- forbids nonlegal professionals to have an ownership or management interest in the law firms;

- bars nonlawyers from sharing legal fees or collecting referral fees;

- requires lawyers to provide clients with a detailed written statement of rights and to obtain written consent to the arrangement;

- spells out in detail when a lawyer will be bound by legal ethics rules when performing nonlegal services;

- reminds lawyers that they cannot allow nonlawyer business associates to impinge on attorneys' professional judgment or take any action that would compromise their ability to protect client confidences; and

- instructs lawyers to refrain from incorporating the names of any nonlawyers or nonlawyer entities into the firm title.[14]

F. Attorney's Fees

---

[14] 22 N.Y. Comp. Codes R. & Regs. §§1200 et seq. "New York Modifies Rule to Authorize Multi disciplinary Business Affiliations," 17 ABA/BNA Manual on Professional Conduct 464 (2001).

This material addresses excessive fees, referral fees, and contingent fees. Discussion of other fee-related issues occurs in Chapter XIII on access to legal services and public interest practice. Analysis in this chapter focuses on inadequacies in both free market and regulatory controls over lawyer-client fee agreements.

The first set of difficulties relates to excessive fees. The *Fordham* case provides an opportunity to ask why courts should second-guess contracts made by consenting adults. Possible answers are that:

(1)   lawyers and clients do not stand at arms' length but rather in a fiduciary relationship, and society has an interest in deterring exploitative agreements to preserve trust in the profession; and

(2)   many clients cannot readily gain access to information about the appropriate value of services.

How to respond to these considerations is problematic, given the vagueness of criteria for determining what are reasonable or excessive fees under DR 2-106, DR 2-107, and Model Rule 1.5. One question to pose in connection with the *Fordham* case is the extent to which clients should have to subsidize a learning experience for an attorney unfamiliar with their kind of problem. Conversely, what sort of premium should clients appropriately pay for an attorney overqualified to handle a simple proceeding? And how much information should clients receive about their attorney's expertise, or lack thereof?

Whether a client's wealth should play a role in assessing the reasonableness of fees is also worth discussing. If, as former Canon 12 and some judicial decisions suggest, a client's lack of resources can justify reduced charges, does it follow that fees for well-off clients can be inflated to subsidize that preferential treatment? The awkwardness of such cross-subsidies may suggest why the Code and Model Rules are silent on the issue of a client's wealth. Whether this reticence is justified may spark a useful debate about the role of Robin-Hood principles and disclosure obligations in setting legal fees.

Lisa Lerman, in "Lying to Clients," 138 *U. Penn. L. Rev.* 659, 709 (1990), quotes one lawyer as follows:

> [M]y billing is certainly influenced by the size and ability of the client to pay. There's pressure to bill . . . at least eight hours a day and I generally bill as much as I can to the richest client [and underbill] clients who can't afford standard rates. . . . It's rough justice.

He added:

> There are rough premiums and discounts that are put into the bills without being disclosed to the client. Not large ones -- not like the New York firms. But when I settled a case I threw down another six hours to a small client, thinking that I under-billed them at other times because they didn't have much money, but I got a good settlement for them. That isn't disclosed.

It is common practice, particularly among large law firms for attorneys to charge "premium" fees -- self-awarded bonuses for achieving results that the firm views as especially favorable. So too, firms will often adjust hours downward if they appear excessive in light of the outcomes achieved. Whether such practices should be explicitly disclosed and whether most firm clients can look out for themselves are matters worth discussing.

The material on referral fees points up other inherent problems in regulation. In an ideal world, it shouldn't be necessary to pay lawyers to forward cases to more competent practitioners. Given the world that currently exists, it is appropriate to ask whether such payments are a necessary concession to attorney self-interest. If that concession is justified, then it also makes sense to ask whether judicial and ethical rules should require that lawyers provide more complete information to clients about the terms of referral fees.

Steven Lubet, in *The Importance of Being Honest*, provides a case study in the problems with referral fees. His example involves Mary Corcoran, whose husband was killed in 1998 while working on a railroad track bed. The railroad offered to settle for $1.4 million, and a friend introduced her to a solo practitioner in Des Plaines, Illinois, Joseph

Dowd, for an opinion on whether to accept. His practice centered on bankruptcy, divorce, and real estate, and he suggested that she consult a personal injury attorney. She proposed Philip Corboy, a leading Chicago attorney, who had known her father in high school. Dowd arranged a meeting, and she signed a contingency fee contract with the Corboy firm, offering to pay 25 percent of any recovery, 40 percent of which would go to Dowd. Afer two years of litigation, the Corboy firm determined that it could not improve on the settlement offer and waived its fee. But Dowd insisted on his share, $140,000 – a large amount for reviewing the file, making a few phone calls, and attending several meetings. An Illinois appellate court sustained his claim, on the theory that if she had wanted a different result, she could have insisted on a "pay for improvement" clause in her retainer agreement. The Illinois Supreme Court declined review. As Lubet notes, the court's opinion neglects to note that she was relying on lawyers to protect her interest and none of them suggested such a clause. *Id.*, at 68-69.

Problem 6 on contingency fees, referral fees, and subsidizing litigation lends itself to role-playing. Students can be asked to assume the perspective of different constituencies on the committee (e.g., a consumer group, the personal injury bar, insurance companies, etc.) Students should consider why only certain fee agreements (contingent, referral) need to be in writing.

As the readings suggest, lawyer-client conflicts of interest can arise with any kind of fee arrangement, so it is useful to ask what regulatory structures can beat minimize any unfairness that might result. It is worth noting that one result of the windfall fees for tort lawyers in some of the large successful class actions has allowed for a kind of balance of power that provides a check on corporate misconduct.[15] The Manhattan Institute's study, "Trial Lawyers, Inc." (2003), estimates that the personal injury bar has annual revenue of about $40 billion. Students can consider both the positive and negative implications of this

---

[15] William Tucker, "Defending Tort Lawyers, Sort of," *The Weekly Standard, Dec. 8, 2003.*

economic power, an issue that will resurface in Chapter XIV's discussion of litigiousness.

The Manhattan Institute proposal described in the Notes on p. 840 offers a useful framework for debate. Professors should explain that the limits on fees when an early offer is accepted (under the proposal, fees will be limited to five or ten percent) are intended as a top estimate of what the lawyer's reasonable hourly fee might be. The point of the proposal is that if the lawyer learns within 60 days of filing a suit that an appropriate settlement offer is available, the case generally involves little work and no risk, and thus charging a premium over and above hourly fees is unjustified. Under the proposal, defendants have an incentive to make a reasonable early offer, because that will often save money. Suppose, for example, that a defendant estimates a liability of $100,000 on a lawsuit, plus $10,000 in legal defense costs. The defendant can make an early offer of $80,000, and it is in the plaintiff's interest to accept it. After all, if the case settles later for $100,000, the plaintiff will recover less than 2/3 of that amount, i.e., $60,000-$65,000, because of the lawyer's 1/3 contingency fee plus case expenses. By accepting the early offer of $80,000, the plaintiff keeps at least $72,000, that is, $80,000 minus the lawyer's maximum-of-10% fee of $8,000.[16] Thus, the early offer and acceptance is in the financial interests of both litigants; moreover, the plaintiff collects the money sooner rather than later. Nor is it unfair to the plaintiff's lawyer, who receives a reasonable hourly fee for a largely risk-free case.

---

[16] Lester Brickman et al., *Rethinking Contingency Fees* 30 (Manhattan Institute 1994). For an overview of problems in contingent fee structures, see Lester Brickman, "The Market for Contingent Fee-Financed Tort Litigation: Is It Price Competitive?," 25 *Cardozo L. Rev.* 65 (2003).

G. Acquiring an Interest in Litigation

The materials on subsidizing litigation raise issues that are likely to increase in significance. As the text indicate, prohibitions on maintenance and champerty grew out of religious and political considerations. In medieval England, the Church disapproved of such practices because they encouraged access to secular courts (which challenged religious authority) and violated precepts on usury. Restrictions on fee arrangements also reduced incentives for corruption or quarrels among feudal lords. American conditions encouraged rules against champerty and maintenance for different reasons. These practices threatened the image of lawyers and appeared likely to encourage litigiousness. Modern prohibitions are generally justified as ways to minimize lawyer-client conflicts of interest. The question worth pursuing in class is whether such practices pose greater difficulties than contingent fees and whether they should be subject to similar regulation.

Judgment Purchase Corporation is an interesting example of what liberalized rules on financing litigation might permit. It buys shares in cases that are on appeal, and screens for the quality of counsel and the ability of defendants to pay an adverse judgement. Students can consider what interests would be served or compromised by allowing lawyers and third parties to play a greater role in financing litigation.

CHAPTER XIII: THE DISTRIBUTION OF LEGAL SERVICES

This chapter focuses on the claim, once summarized by former President Jimmy Carter before the Los Angeles Bar Association, that Americans are "overlawyered and underrepresented."[1] Although such concerns are longstanding, they have also taken on new dimensions and new urgency. Teachers aiming to squeeze this chapter into a limited amount of time can focus primarily on public interest law and pro bono representation, each of which can be fit into a single classroom hour.

A. Litigiousness

The materials in the first section examine conventional assumptions about litigiousness. As the Notes reflect, much of the concern about the recent litigation explosion is factually unsupported. Historical and cross-cultural comparisons between numbers of claims filed or lawyers per capita can also give a distorted picture of incidence of legal disputes. While a brief discussion of all-time favorite frivolous cases can provide welcome comic relief – for this reason we include Dave Barry's column – it is important to emphasize that these cases are neither unique to the American legal system nor a major drain of judicial time.

---

[1] Jimmy Carter, "President Carter's Attack on Lawyers, President Spann's Response, and Chief Justice Burger's Remarks," 64 *A.B.A. J.* 840, 842 (1978).

An interesting illustration of the difficulties of defining "frivolous" is the claim briefly mentioned in the Notes by a fifteen-year old Florida student who sued the individual who stood her up for her first date, and her first prom. She settled for $81.28 (the cost of shoes, hairdo, flowers, and court filing fees). Students may divide over whether such a claim reflects an abuse of judicial process (as the date's mother complained) or whether it sends a useful social signal about the costs of breaching promises.[2] The McDonald's case is another case on which intuitions may differ. Chapter II of Rhode's *Access to Justice* explores ostensibly frivolous cases, including these two, and the general problem of litigiousness in greater detail.

Another amusing case involved a 2008 claim by Charlotte Feeney, who sued for negligence when a package of L'Oreal blonde hair dye turned her into a brunette. The mistake allegedly caused anxiety, depression, and a loss of social life. In her court papers she states: "I was mentally and physically in shock....I don't like myself, I stay home more than ever in my life, I wear hats most of the time....I can never go back to my natural blonde hair. I feel fake about that. Also, blondes do get more attention than brunettes, [and,] of course emotionally I miss that."[3] Feeney claimed that L'Oreal had a duty to put a a warning on every box that the color inside the tube may not be the same as the label. The company denied that the box was mislabeled and claimed that if she had followed directions on the package, she would have done a strand test first, and avoided the mistake. Connecticut Superior Court Judge Richard Gilardi, reportedly not a blonde, dismissed the complaint for lack of evidence suggesting negligence. What is most amusing about the lawsuit is the blog commentary that it generated. One law student's sympathy for the

---

[2] *See* "Quotes," 75 *A.B.A. J.* 30 (1989). It is worth recalling in this context that many claims of sexual harassment were initially dismissed as trivial and a waste of valuable judicial time. For examples, *see* Catharine MacKinnon, *Sexual Harassment of Working Women* (1977); Deborah L. Rhode, *Justice and Gender* 232-35 (1989).

[3] "Case Was Hair Tody, Gone Tomorrow," 34 *Connecticut Law Tribune* 2 (October 13, 2008).

plaintiff, and the pressures she must have faced to be attractive, generated a cascade of negative commentary. One example was : " you are a hoot. I keep telling myself you can't possibly be for real. You are a law student? Wow. The plaintiff here is an idiot... She dyed her hair brown; she can dye it blonde again. Grow up, suck it up, get over it people."

However students come out on particular litigation, their reasoning may underscores a central theme of the chapter – that claims about litigiousness cannot be adequately evaluated in the abstract. It is necessary to ask more specific questions such as those raised in the Notes. In the final analysis, the most critical issue is not how much law and lawyers' services we purchase, but how well we are served by that investment.

The second part of Chapter XIII addresses that issue. The Legal Services Corporation report, new in this edition, and the Notes that follow summarize recent research on the distribution of legal services while raising questions about the elastic and elusive concept of "legal needs." For a more recent update, see Julia Kay's "Deep Cuts Slam Legal Aid," *National Law Journal*, October 27, 2008, at A1, A 17, which chronicles the decline in budgets and IOLTA revenues and the rise in caseloads. Such readings raise the issue that Rhode's book, *Access to Justice,* explores at length: If truly equal justice is not a realistic social aspiration, how can we promote at least adequate access.

D. Public Interest Law

This section explores ethical problems that arise in public interest law in light of its historical background and underlying rationale. Many of these problems involve issues of lawyer accountability and raise traditional concerns about legal activism. Depending on students' backgrounds, it may be useful to summarize certain obvious limitations of democratic institutions and the role of public interest law as a partial corrective. The ACLU's work during the McCarthy era and the NAACP Legal Defense Fund's initiatives during the early civil rights campaign are among the best illustrations.[4] Similar points could be made about more

---

[4] See Henderson, "Is It Worth It," in *From Brown to Bradley: School*

recent efforts concerning women's rights, gay rights, environmental law, consumer law, and so forth.

An interesting way to open discussion is to focus on the definition of public interest. In justifying its support for various public interest legal organizations, a Ford Foundation report maintained: "A central assumption of our democratic society is that the general interest or the common good will emerge out of the conflict of special interests. The public interest law firm seeks to improve this process by giving better representation to certain interests. . . . Providing a voice at the bar for those who could not otherwise make themselves heard can contribute directly to the general welfare by keeping government responsive to the widest possible range of interests.. .."[5]

Yet as the introductory note suggests, underrepresentation cannot be the sole criteria for defining "public interest" representation; an organization representing adults who enjoy sexual activity with children would scarcely qualify. Moreover, the focus on under-representation is politically loaded: the definition excludes a large number of conservative public interest law firms that represent causes (such as property rights, or opposition to government regulation) that could readily attract corporate clients and corporate funding. Conservatives rightly object that confining the label "public interest law" to the political left is tantamount to assuming that conservative causes are not in the public interest.

Desegregation 1954-1974 43 (R. Browning ed. 1975) (noting that before *Brown v. Board of Education*, no black child attended public schools with white students in the deep south. By 1971, almost 44 percent of southern blacks were attending majority white schools).

[5] Ford Foundation, *The Public Interest Law Firm: New Voices for New Constituencies*, 14 (1973).

However, if the concept of public interest requires appeal to principles that attract a consensus across the political spectrum, is it sufficiently determinate to guide decisions about which interests should be voiced? Critics from the left have worried about "fashions in righteousness" and about elitist lawyers imposing their conceptualization of indigents' and minorities' interests.[6] Critics from the right have raised similar accountability issues from a different direction; in their view, public interest attorneys have been out of touch with mainstream values. Jeremy Rabkin notes that a 1983 survey of "public interest" attorneys found that only about two percent voted for Ronald Reagan and four percent for Gerald Ford. When asked to identify individuals that they most admired and looked to for leadership, public interest lawyers placed Bella Abzug and Ralph Nader at the top of the list. Even Fidel Castro outpolled Reagan, three votes to one. Rabkin concludes that "[c]learly, this is not a representative movement, at least not in any obvious statistical way."[7] It is important to note, however, that this poll was conducted years before the advent of major conservative legal policy organizations, such as the Pacific and Rocky Mountain Legal Foundations; it is unlikely that such a poll taken today would yield such skewed results. The point simply is that what counts as public interest law is contested. In conventional usage, the term has come to apply to almost any nonprofit legal organization working on public policy or law reform issues.

Professors interested in a more extended exchange on these issues could assign or summarize the October 6, 2008 speech by Dennis Jacobs, Chief Justice of the Second Circuit Court of Appeals, before the Rochester Federalist Society. It offers a scathing critique of pro bono public interest litigation, particularly "social impact" lawsuits

---

[6] Jean Cahn & Edgar Cahn, "Power to the People or the Profession? -- The Public Interest in Public Interest Law," 79 *Yale L.J.* 1005, 1006 (1970).

[7] Rabkin, "Public Interest Law: Is it Law in the Public Interest?," 8 *Harv. J. of Law & Pub. Pol'y* 341, 343 (1985) (citing Lichter & Rothman, "What Interests the Public and What Interests the Public Interests," *Pub. Opinion*, April-May 1983, at 44).

and claims against the government.

> My point in a nutshell is that much of what we call legal work for the public interest is essentially self-serving. Lawyers use public interest litigation to promote their own agendas, social and political– and (on a wider plane) to promote the power and the role of the legal profession itself. ...Whether a goal is pro bono publico or anti, is often a policy and political judgment. No public good is good for everybody....[I]n pro bono litigation [against the government], the government itself often has a fair claim to representing the public interest– and often a better claim. Everyone in government is accountable to the public...

> Representation of the public interest is high moral ground, the best location in town; so everybody struggles to occupy that space. The field is crowded; the activists and public interest lawyers, the professors and law school clinics, and the pro bono cadres in the law firms... But their standing to speak for the public is self-conferred, nothing more than pretension. As a group, they (of course) do both good and harm. But, unlike public officials, they never have to take responsibility for the outcomes–intended and unintended— of the policy choices they work to impose in the courts.

Jacobs cites several examples. One is a lawsuit by environmental groups that blocked construction of a Louisiana levee, in an area later devastated by Hurricane Katrina. Another is a pro bono case brought by a New York law firm seeking to block eviction of a tenant in public housing who owned several dozen birds that allegedly caused a health hazard. Jacobs also indicts "impact litigation." In his view, the result of such lawsuits is that "[d]emocracy is itself is impaired: The people are distanced from their government; the priorities people vote for are re-ordered; the fisc is opened." And, he adds,

> on those rare occasions when our competitors protest, when elected officials and the public contend that the courts and legal profession have gone too far and have arrogated to themselves powers that belong to other branches of government, to other professions, or that would benefit from other modes of thinking

(such as morals or faith), the Bar forms a cordon around the judiciary and declares that any harsh or effective criticism is an attack on judicial independence.

Jacobs concludes by applauding lawyers who do pro bono work on behalf of "people and institutions that otherwise would be denied essential services and opportunities." That includes "wills for the sick, corporate work for non-profit schools and hospitals, and the representation of pro se litigants whose claims have likely merit." However, he never explains why the examples he criticizes don't fall into those categories, or why non-profit schools or hospitals (many of which can afford counsel) are especially worthy.

In a response to Jacobs' speech, Irvine Law School Dean Erwin Chemerinsky takes issue with the implicit assumption that pro bono work reflects a liberal political agenda. Much of this work, Chemerinksy argues,"has no ideological content, such as in helping a victim of domestic violence get an essential restraining order or assisting a child with learning disabilities receive an adequate education." Some work is conservative, and some impact litigation is essential to address "systemic violations of the Constitution that otherwise go unremedied," such as school segregation or inhumane prison conditions. According to Chemerinsky, speeches like Jacobs do a disservice by giving lawyers and law firms a convenient rationalization for failing to provide crucial volunteer assistance.[8]

E. Subsidized Legal Services

A natural focus for discussing this section is the Legal Services

---

[8]Erwin Chemerinsky, "Not a Self- Serving Activity," *National Law Journal,* October27, 2008, at A22. Both Chemerinsky's column and Jacobs' speech are available on the National Law Journal website, www.nlj.com.

Corporation Act amendments of 1996 and the *Velazquez* case. Professors may point out that the 1996 law was enacted at a high-water mark of conservative dominance of Congress, soon after the Republican Party obtained control of both houses, and its leadership published the "Contract With America." Unlike the early 1980s, when efforts to abolish the Legal Services Corporation met with powerful resistance from the legal profession, LSC supporters in 1996 were dissuaded from too activist a stance in opposing restrictions out of concern that the alternative would be outright abolition. Indeed, many proponents of the LSC opposed legal challenges such as *Velazquez* on that ground. The question that supporters of the LSC confronted was whether the 1996 Act restrictions would cripple LSC recipients' ability to practice law ethically and effectively.

The major problem is that the Act does not merely prohibit using LSC funds for unauthorized activities. Rather, it forbids LSC recipients from engaging in those activities, even if they are not using LSC funds. The immediate effect is to force legal services providers to choose between accepting the restrictions or giving up all federal subsidies. In practice, this meant that some providers split into two separate organizations – one that receives LSC funds and abides by the restrictions, and one that does without LSC funds but undertakes broader activities. Other organizations have curtailed their activities either to fit within the restrictions or to fit within a reduced budget, which typically requires downsizing staff and devoting more effort to fundraising from other sources.

ABA Formal Opinion 96-399 provoked controversy at the time. Many LSC supporters argued that the role of the ABA was to state forthrightly that the restrictions made it impossible for LSC lawyers to practice law ethically. The ABA committee attempted rather to find some way of enabling LSC recipients to comply with both statutory and ethical requirements. The Opinion reached several controversial conclusions, including for example, that LSC recipients may need to warn clients at initial interviews about the restrictions, so that clients know that incarceration or a change in immigrant status may make them ineligible for help. Critics asked rhetorically what kind of client-lawyer trust relationship could be established if that was the content of the first interview. Alan Houseman's article, cited on p.891 n. 65, discusses

195

many of these issues.

The 2008 election of a Democratic administration has encouraged a push to repeal some or all of the LSC restrictions. For updates on this effort and activism around creation of a "civil Gideon" right to counsel, see the website of Brennan Center for Justice, htp://www.brennancenter.org.

Underlying the debate about federal funding and restrictions are broader questions of public policy. One issue worth pursuing involves the claim by some of the first organizers of legal services, as well as contemporary commentators, that subsidized assistance helps legitimate our legal and political structures. Critics from the left such as Richard Abel challenge this claim.[9] Citing a wide array of studies, Abel notes that most of the eligible poverty population is ignorant of the availability of legal assistance, that many who are eligible do not receive significant help from overworked offices, and those who come in contact with the legal system have a less favorable impression of its fairness than those who do not. Under Abel's analysis, if legal aid serves a legitimating function, then it does so for the economically and socially privileged, who want to convince themselves that "those privileges are justified or better yet, that they have no privileges." By alleviating some of the worst inequalities, poverty law programs, like other welfare initiatives, "may distract attention from the overwhelming inequality that remains."[10] To take an obvious example, providing a small fraction of the poor with lawyers and procedural protection in landlord/tenant disputes fails to address the most fundamental problem of widespread inability to afford decent housing or to enforce health and safety building code standards.

Students sympathetic to this claim should be asked to work through its logical implications. Would they prefer a system of no legal services in order to heighten the misery of the poor and foment revolutionary change? It is worth noting that Abel does not take this position; he argues for massive subsidies and a required post-graduate

---

[9] Richard Abel, "Law Without Politics: Legal Aid Under Advanced Capitalism," 32 *U.C.L.A. L. Rev.* 474, 601-02 (1985).

[10] Id. at 603-04.

internship program for all prospective lawyers. But, for reasons he acknowledges, simply enhancing access to lawyers will not equalize legal resources between the "haves" and "have-nots." His earlier analysis thus raises questions about whether greater subsidies would risk further camouflaging the power disparities he condemns.

However that issue is resolved, there remain substantial practical difficulties in allocating scarce legal resources. Such difficulties are in some sense analogous to those involved in apportioning limited medical resources. **Problems 1-3** address different dimensions of this issue and raise questions about what criteria should guide allocative decisions and who should decide.

The practical obstacles to enhancing client control underscore some of the same concerns discussed in Chapter XI on paternalism. To most students, the Legal Services Corporation guidelines in Problem 2 look fine in the abstract; the problem lies in implementation. In some measure, mandates of adequate client participation presuppose precisely what is lacking – an informed and cohesive community among eligible recipients. How legal services lawyers can best empower clients when the result may be to challenge lawyers' own desires for autonomy is a question worth further discussion.

An increasing array of materials on community lawyering address these themes. The goal of many contemporary poverty lawyers is to create effective local participants in policy making processes and empower poor clients to help themselves through cooperative action.[11] An interesting example is the strategy of time dollars, which people can earn by assisting others and can spend on subsidized assistance, including legal services. For example, a local community development organization negotiated with a private firm to obtain legal services in exchange for residents' work in neighborhood clean-up projects, tutoring, escort services for the elderly, and so forth. Part of the point of such arrangements is to alter the relationship between lawyers and clients from one of "subordination and dependency," to "parity, mutuality, and

---

[11]   Michael Diamond, "Community Lawyering, Revisiting the Old Neighborhood," 32 *Colum. Human Rights L. Rev.* 67 (2000).

reciprocity."[12]

F. Alternative Dispute Resolution

Professors may wish to combine this section with the material on mediation ethics from Chapter VIII. The issues are fairly straightforward and the material cited in the notes should be more than adequate to address any questions that teachers might have in class preparation.

G. Pro Bono Representation

If it can ever be credibly said that the material "teaches itself," this section qualifies. Students invariably have strong views on required service, and in some classes teachers will have to make the arguments on one or another side to balance out the discussion. The most common objections to pro bono requirements are that it will lead to incompetent representation of the poor by lawyers unfamiliar with their special problems, and that it is unfair to make lawyers donate in-kind assistance when other occupations have no such obligation. A standard reply to the former argument is that pro bono work on matters such as uncontested divorces and landlord/tenant disputes is usually rudimentary enough that any trained lawyer should be able to do a respectable job, and rules permitting financial contributions in lieu of direct service can minimize efficiency concerns. A standard reply to the "why only lawyers" is to argue that other occupations with a state-enforced monopoly over crucial services should assume similar obligations. An alternative argument is that lawyers enjoy special privileges that carry special obligations and that access to law provides unique and fundamental safeguards for individual rights and democratic processes. This discussion can be combined with the material on law school pro bono programs in Chapter XVI.

---

[12] Edgar Cahn, "Coproducing Justice," 5 U. D.C. L. Rev. 105 (2000).

CHAPTER XIV: ADMISSION TO THE BAR

Most students are interested in the regulatory issues surrounding admission for the obvious reason: they have an immediate and personal stake in how the structure operates. The Hurst excerpt provides a useful historical dimension. The range of qualifications over time are worth noting: for example, the Scottish bar's desire for fencing and dancing skills; the British bar's categorical exclusion of Catholics, journalists, and tradesmen; and the American bar's rejection of women whose "natural delicacy" made them unfit for forensic strife.

The potential arbitrariness of contemporary examination and character procedures are also worth noting. Given the difficulties of predicting future immoral conduct, it is useful to press students about what functions the character inquiry serves and what conduct they personally would find disabling. An interesting case beyond those noted in Problem 1 could involve the admissibility of a victim of unrequited love. As indicated in Chapter XV on discipline, Burton Pugach, a New York attorney, hired three "thugs" to throw lye in the face of the woman who rejected him after learning he was married. After serving 14 years in prison for the crime, Pugach married the woman whom he had blinded and disfigured. According to a *New York Times* account, she hoped the bar would readmit her husband because "he shouldn't be punished into the grave."[1] The bar did not, and he worked as a paralegal, exhibiting what was widely viewed as a "story of redemption." Then, ten years later, he was arrested for harassing and sexually abusing a woman with whom he had a five-year affair. She claimed he had threatened to kill her when she broke off their relationship. His wife, who apparently had forgiven him (again) was scheduled to testify as a character witness.[2]

---

[1] "Love Story: Part II," N.Y. Times, Feb. 22, 1987, at 26.

[2] Norimitsu Onishi, "A Tangled Affair of the Heart," *N.Y. Times*, April 21, 1997, at B8.

Variations on such facts can make for an interesting discussion. Students who believe that character inquiries should be strictly limited to evidence relating to professional conduct are often uncomfortable with admitting an attorney whose crime appears so brutal (Pugach's stated desire was to prevent the woman from being attractive to anyone else). On the other hand, students who wish to exclude such attorneys for some extended period can be pressed for a rationale that includes a limiting principle. Presumably, lawyers like Pugach are unlikely to replicate their violence with clients and their disrespect for law has already triggered substantial punishment under the criminal code. The question thus becomes whether excluding such individuals from the bar serves independent societal objectives, apart from preserving the bar's image. A celebrated comparison case involving reinstatement is *In re Hiss*, 368 Mass. 447, 333 N.E.2d 429 (1975), in which the Massachusetts' Supreme Court readmitted Alger Hiss despite his continued refusal to admit guilt for the perjury offense that prompted his imprisonment and disbarment.

Mental health inquiries are a controversial topic that is likely to generate further litigation and bar rule-making. The issue lends itself to role playing, with students representing various constituencies concerned with regulatory policy. Jon Bauer's article, cited in the footnotes, gives a particularly detailed account of the flaws in the current process and a plausible, albeit expensive, alternative. Other cases that can make interesting hypothetical problems are as follows.

In *In re Zbiegien*, 433 N.W.2d 871 (Minn. 1979), an applicant was admitted to the bar despite plagiarizing a paper under circumstances of stress, including his wife's illness. This case could be compared to that of Anne Laura Bell Lamb, 776 P.2d 665 (Cal. 1989), discussed in Chapter XV, where an attorney was disbarred for taking the bar exam for her husband despite evidence of illness, extreme stress, and threats of domestic violence if she did not take the test.

In *Matter of Anonymous*, 549 N.E. 2d 472 (N.Y. 1989), the court held that bar examiners may reject an applicant because of the inability to handle personal finances so long as bankruptcy is not the reason for rejection. Students can consider whether the applicants in these cases could have avoided difficulty by waiting to declare bankruptcy until just after their admission to the bar. If so, what does that suggest about the double standard for admission and discipline?

CHAPTER XV: DISCIPLINE AND MALPRACTICE

A. Introduction

This chapter examines methods of regulating lawyers' conduct from both descriptive and prescriptive vantages. The discussion seeks to raise questions both about the primary objectives of professional oversight and the ability of the current disciplinary and malpractice system to fulfill them.

B. Regulatory Structure and Standards and
C. Disciplinary Sanctions

The premise of self-regulation is that only lawyers can or should assess other lawyers' conduct. Problem 1 and the materials on reporting disciplinary violations draw this premise into questio-n. *Himmel, Wieder v. Skala*, and *Bohatch* are quite straightforward to teach.. It is worth noting that Himmel would not have been obligated to report Casey under Model Rule 8.3 because the information came from information protected as confidential under Rule 1.6. In answer to **Question 2, p.976**, the most obvious way of distinguishing *Wieder* from *Bohatch* is that Wieder was an associate -- hence, an employee – of the law firm, whereas Bohatch was a partner. The Texas court seemed particularly moved by the thought that partners cannot be compelled to maintain the partnership with each other. The counter-argument is that finding for Bohatch would not compel them to maintain the partnership – it would simply require them to pay damages for terminating it.

Another important point to raise in connection with these cases is the obligation of law firm partners under Model Rule 5.1(a) to "make reasonable efforts to ensure that the firm has in effect measures giving reasonable assurance that all lawyers in the firm conform to the Rules of Professional Conduct." Presumably, firing lawyers to retaliate for their conforming to the Rules of Professional Conduct would violate Rule 5.1(a), and thus subject the partner to discipline. However, neither New York nor Texas has adopted Rule 5.1(a).

Even if whistleblower protections are in effect, it is questionable that many lawyers will inform on their colleagues. The low percentage of disciplinary complaints arising from lawyers (l0 percent) is some indication of prevailing norms.

A question worth exploring is whether to focus on altering or accommodating these norms. Should more efforts be made to enforce reporting requirements in cases like *Himmel*? Or should the rules be changed to demand only that lawyers provide evidence requested by a tribunal? If jurisdictions pursue the latter strategy, the materials suggest ways for disciplinary agencies to expand other sources of information.

Research and reform efforts have underscored the need for both internal and external initiatives in the disciplinary system. Substantial progress can occur through the strategies noted in the text: additional resources and professional staff; greater public disclosure and outreach; more reliance on fairly designed informal dispute resolution procedures, and so forth. However, as experience in California also suggests, the way to achieve such changes is often through external pressure from the press, the legislature, or a consumer protection official such as a bar monitor.

Proposals to shift disciplinary functions to an agency outside the bar's formal or informal control merit serious consideration. Although the profession has historically opposed such efforts, the trend toward co-regulation in other countries (discussed on pp. 984-85) may push in that direction.

For those interested in additional material, Richard Abel's new book, *Lawyer in the Dock,* offers a rich empirical analysis of the disciplinary system at work in New York and California. His focus is on lawyers from small firm and solo practice charged with neglect, overcharging and overzealous representation, who make up a large percentage of those receiving sanctions. Most of these lawyers "drift into such conduct" and rationalize their abuses ("everyone does it"). His analysis, coupled with a review of research on white collar crime and medical malpractice, suggests various reforms, most of which are suggested by material in the casebook (mandatory malpractice insurance, a clients' bill of rights, public access to disciplinary and malpractice complaints). More controversial proposals are to ban solo practice (which leaves struggling lawyers without adequate backup coverage), and review panels to provide clients with low cost second opinions about lawyers' proposed courses of action and fees.

D. Sanctions

Issues surrounding sanctions generally provoke heated debate. The cases involving Clinton, Cooper, Reich, and Perkins pose interesting questions of general versus specific deterrence and suggest a number of questions for class discussion. If the point of discipline is public protection and not punishment, should it matter whether an individual has suffered enough? Critics often complain that the bar seldom seeks sanctions against lawyers from prestigious firms or high-level public officials. Are the cases involving Clinton and Perkins examples? How important is securing public confidence in the profession or in the disciplinary process?

Leslie Levin's article offers a comprehensive summary of problems in the sanctioning process: leniency, bias, indeterminacy, and inconsistency. She offers some instructive examples, and adds details concerning the Cooper case. There, a hearing panel composed of elite lawyers imposed an unduly light sanction and the reviewing court made no reference to the standards it used and gave no reason for treating Cooper more leniently than other lawyers with criminal convictions. Levin also notes that some New York lawyers who attempted to defraud their partners or employers have received more severe sentences than those who defrauded their clients. As Levin notes, "who you are and who you know" may be as important as "what you have done" in determining sanctions. Levin's overview highlights structural problems in the process, including both undue bar influence and ambiguities in how to weigh particular factors. Even in states with disciplinary systems that are nominally independent of the organized bar, such systems often rely on the profession for financial support, volunteers, and appointments to disciplinary panels.   Such ties often inhibit decisionmakers from imposing adequate sanctions.[1]

---

[1] Leslie C. Levin, "The Emperor's Clothes and Other Tales About the Standards for Imposing Lawyers' Discipline Sanctions," *Am. U. L.*

A related question is whether such concerns are equally relevant for conduct occurring outside the scope of professional employment. That issue can be addressed in contexts such as those involving violence, consensual sex, drugs, and tax evasion. Students who believe that the sole function of the disciplinary process is to protect clients should be pressed on how they feel, or how they think most clients would feel, about allowing practice by attorneys who murder their wife or commit sodomy with children. Compare for example, *In re Nevell*, 704 P.2d 1332, 1333 (Cal. 1985) (rejecting referee's recommendation of two-and-one-half year suspension for man convicted of killing his wife after a dispute concerning marital infidelity); *Muskingum County Bar Association v. Workman*, 477 N.E.2d 632 (Ohio 1985) (one-year suspension for attorney who fractured nose of woman with whom he was having extramarital affair); *People v. Grenemeyer*, 745 P.2d 1027 (Colo. 1987) (disbarment for attorney who engaged in sexual conduct with a fifteen year old boy); *In re Adonizzio*, 469 A.2d 432 (N.J. 1984) (three month suspension for male attorney convicted of sexual offense involving minor); *Matter of Cambial*, 322 N.J. 224 (1987) (finding sexual assault against a male minor to be unrelated to legal work and allowing attorney who was undergoing treatment to retain a practice restricted for four years to title examinations).

By contrast, students who feel that disrespect for law is an adequate justification for bar sanctions should be pressed on cases involving civil disobedience, draft resistance, or criminal homosexual acts with consenting adults such as those cited in Rhode's moral character study. Are students comfortable with the philosophy articulated by the court in *State v. Postorino*, 193 N.W.2d 1, 4 (Wis. 1972): "a lawyer is a professional twenty-four hours a day . . . ."? Do they agree with the court in *In re Boudreau,* 815 So. 2d 76 (La. 2002), cited p. 994, which involved a lawyer who served 21 months in prison for bringing sexually explicit child pornography magazines back from Europe? In imposing disbarment, the court analogized the conduct to making unwanted sexual demands on clients, which had previously served to

---

Rev. 1(1998).

justify that ultimate sanction. An interesting addition to the facts in the Pugach case is discussed above, in this Manual's   chapter on admission.

Another interesting, although off-color, case for those who want to wake the class up is *In re Inglimo*, 740 N.W.2d 125 (Wisc. 2007) in which the court suspended for three years a lawyer who had mismanaged trust accounts, taken drugs with clients, and persuaded one client to share his girlfriend in a menage a trois with the lawyer. The most interesting part of the discussion is the court's rejection of the finding by the state's Office of Lawyer Regulation that the lawyer violated Wisconsin Rule 1.8(k)(2) banning sexual relations with clients. In the court's view, the three way act did not violate the rule since the client was only observing, not touching, the lawyer.

A similarly colorful case involved a hypothetical put to The Ethicist in the Sunday *New York Times Magazine* ("Sexual Ethics," Aug 26, 2007, at 18). "I am a lawyer. During a first date with another lawyer, we had sex and I wore a condom. Days later, when I came down with a bad fever and couldn't determine the cause, she revealed that she had genital herpes. A judgeship will soon open up in her county, and she's a near lock for it. But if I report her lapse of sexual ethics, I doubt that the selection committee will pick her. Should I ?"
Ethicist Randy Cohen responds :"You should not. No doubt your paramour acted dreadfully. She should have told you that she had herpes and let you decide whether you wished to accept the risk. But the selection committee is not choosing a role model for the kids or someone to ride the express elevator to heaven; it seeks a person who will excel at a particular job. I do not believe that this sort of sexual misconduct correlates with an ability to be a good judge. " Cohen distinguishes private conduct like belonging to the Ku Klux Klan or using racist slurs which would "not inspire confidence in his or her ability to dispense equal justice to all. But being unscrupulous in bed does not presage being inept on the bench, and so you should keep this demoralizing episode to yourself . And your doctor."

Obviously, other countries confront similar issues. Professors interested in how Australia, Canada, and New Zealand grapple with lawyer's personal (rather than professional) misconduct could consult Duncan Webb & Alice Woolley, "Screamin' Mo Sychuck: Nefarious

Conduct and the Fit and Proper Person Test" (forthcoming, 2009). Examples that they discuss include lawyers who: murdered his wife in a fit of rage; misled conservation officials about whether he had killed a grizzly bear without a license; engaged in sexual misconduct with minor girls; neglected farm animals; and solicited sexual acts in a public place. At issue in all these cases is how to weigh concerns such as protection for clients, the reputation of the profession, and evidence of remorse and rehabilitation.

The *Clinton* case is a useful case history for raising these issues. Ethics experts who disagreed about what sanctions were appropriate for Clinton also disagreed about whether he "got off easy." According to Michael Flaherty, president of the Association of Public Responsibility Lawyers (an organization of discipline defense attorneys), "It's a pretty heavy penalty." Since the actions did not occur in the course of an attorney-client relationship and there were no aggravating factors in Clinton's background, disbarment appeared excessive. By contrast, other defense attorneys specializing in disciplinary cases believed that Clinton got a "fabulous deal." Given his earning potential, $25,000 was an inconsequential sum.[2]

---

[2] Daniel A. Shaw, "A Bar Divided: Did Clinton Get Off Easy?" *San Francisco Daily J.*, Jan 22, 2001.

Two further issues related to sanctions are also worth discussing: whether disbarment should be permanent; and whether prosecutors should target lawyers guilty of egregious misconduct. As the chapter notes, states vary considerably in their approach to reinstatements. Pennsylvania is one of the most liberal; it readmits over three quarters of disbarred attorneys who apply. And it makes some disturbing mistakes. A case in point involved George Machina, who was disbarred for neglect and misappropriations, and then, after readmittance, engaged in similar misconduct. His victims the second time around included an elderly couple. His negligence caused dismissal of a serious medical malpractice claim, and it took four years after the couple filed a complaint for the bar to complete disbarment proceedings. In the interim, he continued to practice and confidentiality requirements prevented any warnings to other potential victims.[3] Additional examples of exploitation of vulnerable elderly clients that might warrant prosecution or permanent disbarment are profiled in a *Washington Post* expose of the D.C. guardian system.[4] Victims included a nursing home resident who was forced to leave because an attorney neglected to pay her bills and who ended up without electricity and telephone service for similar reasons. Meanwhile, he expropriated over $10,000 of her funds, mishandled funds for seven other clients, and repeatedly failed to appear or file reports to courts. Students can consider whether disbarment with the possibility of reinstatement is a sufficient sanction.

E. Competence and Malpractice

Schatz (pp. 1018-19) is perhaps the best-known case rejecting the liability of lawyers for participating in client frauds. To put the decision into context, it is important to realize two things: First, as Professor Hazard notes, only a handful of courts agree with *Schatz* that a lawyer cannot be held liable for fraud to a person who is not the

---

[3] Chris Other & Brad Bunted, "Disbarment Not the End for Lawyers," *Pittsburgh Tribune Review*, Feb. 17, 2003, at 1.

[4] Carol D. Linage & Sarah Cohen, "Under Court, Vulnerable Become Victims: Attorneys Who Ignored Clients or Misspent Funds Rarely Sanctioned," *Washington Post*, June 15, 2003, at A1.

lawyer's client.[5] Second, it is very likely that the Fourth Circuit Court of Appeals was unreceptive to the Schatzes' claim because it arose in the context of securities fraud, and the court (like many others) has become concerned that securities litigation has become an arena for gold-digging.[6] Nevertheless, the Court does hold, strikingly, "that a lawyer or law firm cannot be liable for the representations of a client, even if the lawyer incorporates the client's misrepresentations into legal documents or agreements necessary to closing the transaction." The court's language is as troubling as its conclusion. It claims that the Schatzes' complaint against Weinberg & Green is "only that they failed to tattle on their client for misrepresenting his personal financial condition."[7] Students can discuss what limits on lawyers' malpractice liability might be more appropriate.

CHAPTER XVI: LEGAL EDUCATION

We have not structured this chapter around problems because our experience suggests that students and professors generally prefer to talk about their own understanding of what the problems are. Many faculty may use this chapter in a final class devoted to reflections on

---

[5] Geoffrey C. Hazard, Jr., "The Privity Requirement Reconsidered," 37 *S. Texas L. Rev.* 967, 970 (1996).

[6] Arguably, the Fourth Circuit misunderstood the nature of the Schatz's claim, which was not that Weinberg & Green had committed malpractice against them but rather that Weinberg & Green had participated in securities fraud against them.

[7] 943 F.2d, at 491.

legal ethics instruction in law school, which students will rightly understand as a salutary effort to encourage course critique. We have, however, tried to provide reading with enough range and depth to provoke discussion beyond the usual laundry list of personal grievances. In structuring that discussion, it is often helpful to begin with questions about the most critical functions of legal education, such as learning to identify, analyze, and research legal issues; developing practice-related skills; and reinforcing (or questioning) professional norms and values. Discussion can then center on how professional schools could better prepare students for a life in the law.

It is also interesting to ask students to recall why they wanted to become lawyers and what they said in law school application forms on that point. (Some individuals may need to consult admission office files since the stated reasons may not be memorable). Discussion can then turn to whether the reasons have changed and if so, why.

The usefulness of large lecture or quasi-Socratic approaches will generally spark a heated discussion. Kennedy's diatribe will hit home with students on the left, while others are likely to find it irritating. Kronman's eloquent defense of the case method provides an important counterweight to Kennedy. We suggest focusing discussion on the two questions following his excerpt. Excerpts from the Carnegie Foundation report, *Educating Lawyers,* new to this edition, raises important questions about the effectiveness of legal education in teaching practical skills, providing feedback, and reinforcing professional responsibility.

The criticisms raised by feminist and critical race theorists provide a useful agenda for discussion. Recent controversies surrounding the law school accreditation process can also point up some of the practical policy questions at stake. Additional material of interest could include Chapter Seven on Legal Education from Rhode's *In the Interest of Justice* and a recent exchange on accreditation in the *National Law Journal.* It was sparked by law professor George Shepard's claim that the process operates to exclude racial minorities because it requires use of LSAT scores (which disproportionately exclude black students) and requires expenditures that inflate tuition costs. John Sebert, the ABA's consultant on legal education, defended the system and Michael Coyne, Joseph Devlin and Peter Malaguli from the Massachusetts School of

211

Law responded. See "The ABA's Dual System," *Nat'l Law J.*, Aug. 6, 2001, at A23.

Professors may also wish to spend time focusing on *Grutter v. Bollinger*. Although the decision was widely perceived as a victory for affirmative action, it is worth noting the concern that some supporters have raised about the Court's opinion. For example, Jerry Parkinson, Dean of Wyoming College of Law, endorses the determination that diversity is a compelling interest that can justify the use of race in admissions. But he also was disappointed that the Court did not engage in the kind of "penetrating critical analysis" of the role of LSAT scores that would "force all of us to undertake a serious reexamination of our admission practices."[1] As he notes, expert testimony in the case found that the correlation between LSAT scores and first year grades was only 16-20 percent, and that taking an LSA preparation course improved an applicant's score by approximately seven points. The rationale for relying on such an imperfect measure of ability was simply that no other criteria had more predictive power. On this basis, the Court concluded that Michigan had sufficiently considered race-neutral alternatives but had rejected them because they would "lower admission standards and force the school to become a "much different institution."[2] But, as Parkinson notes, it might be a better institution. To assume that lower scores necessarily translates into "lower standards" presupposes an overly narrow definition of merit. A de-emphasis on the members would, as he notes, benefit many deserving applicants not just members of underrepresented groups. "And . . . it may benefit the legal *profession* as well. Barbara Grutter is described in the Supreme Court opinion as a white Michigan resident who applied to the Law School in 1996 with a 3.8 grade average and 161 LSAT score. But who *is* she? Is she the type of *person* we want in law school and in the legal profession? Surely she cannot be defined by her 'numbers'."[3]

Some professors may wish to include more of the specific

---

[1] Jerry R. Parkinson, "Admissions After Grutter," 35 *U. Tol. L. Rev.* 159 (2003).

[2] *Id.*, at 163.

[3] *Id.*, at 166.

critiques of Richard Sander's study condemning affirmative action, including David Wilkins' claim that over the course of the career, the prestige of law school attended matters more than graduates' GPA.

Wendy Moore's 2008 book, *Reproducing Racism,* offers rich detail about the racial dynamics of two unnamed elite law schools. Her interviews offer a window into white students' concerns about affirmative action (e.g. that economically privileged blacks with low LSATs get into elite schools, that liberal professors of color won't be fair in grading, and that whites are made to feel guilty about wrongs they had no role in committing). She also explores black students' experiences of racial bias (e. g. white students' unwillingness to schedule informal events at bars where minorities felt welcome, or professors' avoidance of discussions of racism even in constitutional law classes where equal protection issues should be central). However, Moore offers almost no reform agenda (other than getting more academics of color into leadership positions), and that of itself could suggest discussion.

The details concerning AutoAdmit and the Top 14 contest make excellent teaching material. The contest site almost crashed from heavy traffic and Cohen felt he deserved a "golden star" for getting contest owner to allow him to shut down the Top 14 out of privacy concerns. One of the Yale students ridiculed on Auto Admit, although a Phi Beta Kappa graduate with law journal publications got no offers from the 16 firms she interviewed with and ended up taking a semester off from school. In a posting March 9, 2007 on MS JD, one of the students discloses the threads that Google searches will reveal as a result of the AutoAdmit postings: "_____ fucked her way into Yale," "_____, why did you have an abortion,""_____NUDE PHOTOS,"" _____anal sex gang bang," etc. The threads were a topic during her summer job interviews. Nonetheless, she believes that it is an "inherently good thing" that the site lets "EVERYTHING in." Dean Elena Kagan from Harvard Law School (which had some of its students posted) urged boycotts of this "new and highly efficient mechanism for malicious gossip (March 13, 2007) and Jack Balkin urged site administrators to post a statement that such conduct was "unacceptable."

In the George Washington controversy discussed in the questions following the FAIR decision, the school decided to let the military employers attend but required posting of a disclaimer indicating that they discriminate in violation of GW's policy, and permitted Lambda members to protest outside the event as long as they did not disrupt the activities. Joan Schauffer's article analyzes the relevant legal precedents and concludes that student groups should not have the right to invite these employers. In her view, the only protected interest at stake is students right to receive information and that right would not be foreclosed by denying a campus invitation; students could readily receive the information from the Web or from visits to nearby offices.[4]

It is often highly effective, although not altogether risk-free, to close the semester by asking students what they wish had been different about their legal education (apart from the cost), and what they think that they, as alumni, bar leaders, or legislators, could do to make such changes happen.

A further topic for consideration is the competitive and stressful nature of the law school experience, and the high rates of depression and substance abuse among students. Since some individuals may find it difficult to discuss these issues in a large class, this edition moves material on this subject to the manual. It appears as an appendix to this chapter to facilitate xeroxing as a supplement. We also include a possible class exercise on diversity that one of us has found quite

---

[4]For discussion of arguments opposing the Don't Ask policy but supporting the Supreme Court's ruling see Thaddeus Hoffmeister, "Good Ruling, Bad Policy," *Nat'l L. J.*, March 27, 2006 (noting that between 65% to 79% of Americans support allowing gays to openly serve in the military, that 76% of potential military recruits reported that lifting the ban would have "no effect" on their decision, and that the discharge of 10,000 service personnel had resulted in losses that were hard to fill).

successful, even in a fairly large class.

Discussion of the Professional Responsibility course can center around the question, quoted from a *Student Lawyer* article, of why the course is "hard to teach, disappointing to take, and often presented to vacant seats or vacant minds." The article described a class (in an amusing passage not quoted in the text):

> Fifteen minutes into the class precisely one student has spoken. The rest, with edgy apprehension, look down at the floor, the desks, their books – everywhere but at their guest teacher . . . .
>
> Although it sounds like a high school session on personal hygiene, these averted faces actually belong to a class on professional responsibility at an American law school.[5]

We hope that classes that use our text are not subject to this kind of criticism.

---

[5] Dale C. Moss, "Out of Balance: Why Can't Law Schools Teach Ethics?" *Student Lawyer*, Oct. 1991, at 19.

APPENDIX

The Law School Culture and Quality of Life

A final set of criticisms involves the competitive and stressful aspects of law school culture. Some commentators have singled out conventional grading structures as particularly demoralizing. T.S. Eliot claimed that April was the cruelest month, but for law students and law teachers that is far from true. As Jay Feinman and Marc Feldman suggest, it is the December/January, May/June cycle that bring forth massive despair via "blue book blues."[1] Exams graded on a predetermined curve often function less to teach than to rank. Many students receive little constructive feedback throughout the semester or on the final product. For them, the grading process seems more a service law schools perform for the benefit of legal employers, rather than a part of the educational mission. Students who do not excel in the limited skills that exams measure frequently suffer significant alienation and stress.

---

[1] Jay Feinman & Marc Feldman, "Pedagogy and Politics," 73 *Go. L. J.* s875 (1985). See also Kissam, *supra* note 26, at 26, 263-66.

One of the most sophisticated empirical efforts to measure such stress found that law school significantly increased symptoms such as obsessive-compulsive behavior, depression, anxiety, hostility, paranoid fantasies, social alienation, and isolation. Depending on the symptoms, 20%-40% of students in any given law school class report significant stress.[2] In another broad-based survey, 11 percent of students reported abusing alcohol since entering law school.[3] According to some prominent researchers, the problem is that "the law school educational process itself affects individuals rather than that certain types of individuals choosing to enter law school overreact to the process because of their unique and rare vulnerabilities."[4] Although prospective law students do not differ from the population generally in their mental health, current students do differ. For example, their rates of depression are about three times higher than the population generally.[5]

Although the exact causes of stress are difficult to measure, recent research generally identifies the following factors:

1) excessive workloads and times management problems;

2) chronically high student-faculty ratios leading to limited interactions and feedback;

3) inadequate attention to student interpersonal skills;

---

[2] Andrew H. Benjamin et al., "The Role of Legal Education in Producing Psychological Distress Among Law Students and Lawyers," 1986 *Am. B. Found.* 225, 246, 248-52; Ann. L. Iijima, "Lessons Learned, Legal Education and Law Student Dysfunction," 48 *J. Legal Educ.* 524 (1998).

[3] "Report of the AALS Special Committee on Problems of Substance Abuse in Law Schools," 44 *J. Legal Educ.* 35, 44 (1994).

[4] Benjamin et al., *supra* note 2, at 247. See also Iijima, *supra* note 2.

[5] Benjamin, et al., *supra* note 2.

4) inadequate information, counseling, and treatment programs concerning psychological and substance abuse problems; and

5) inadequate assurances of confidentiality for students who would benefit from counseling and treatment.[6]

QUESTIONS

1. What changes in law school culture would be most helpful in improving the educational experience and preparing prospective lawyers for future demands in practice?

2. Under what, if any circumstances should law schools be required to disclose information about honor code violations, or substance abuse and mental health problems to the state bar?

3. If you had a close friend in law school with psychological or substance abuse problems, how would you respond? How should schools respond?

EXERCISE

Students should break into small groups or "identity groups" along lines of race, ethnicity, gender, sexual orientation, etc. Members of each group should discuss:

- how their background has affected their law school

---

[6] Report of the AALS Special Committee, *supra* note 3. See also Lawrence S. Krieger, "What We're Not Telling Law Students – and Lawyers – That They Really Need to Know: Some Thoughts-In-Action Toward Revitalizing the Profession from its Roots," 13 . *L. & Health* 15 (1998-99).

experience;

- how their institution has responded to diversity-related issues;

- what changes they would like to see in legal education in general and in their school in particular.

Notes

Notes

Notes